IN PERPETUITY THROUGHOUT THE UNIVERSE

Eric Overmyer

357 W 20th St., NY NY 10011
212 627-1055

IN PERPETUITY THROUGHOUT THE UNIVERSE
© Copyright 1989 by Eric Overmyer

First printing: January 1989
ISBN: 0-88145-065-0

Design by Marie Donovan
Word processing done in WordMarc Composer Plus.
Set in Palatino using Xerox Ventura Publisher and Printware 7201Q output.
Printed on acid-free paper and bound by BookCrafters, Inc., Chelsea, MI.

ABOUT THE AUTHOR

Eric Overmyer is an Associate Artist of Center Stage, Baltimore.

Plays: NATIVE SPEECH (*Broadway Play Publishing, 1984*), ON THE VERGE (*Broadway Play Publishing, 1986*), and IN A PIG'S VALISE (*Published in the collection* SEVEN DIFFERENT PLAYS, *Broadway Play Publishing, 1988*).

TV: *St Elsewhere, The Days and Nights of Molly Dodd, The "Slap" Maxwell Story.*

Radio: *Kafka's Radio* (WNYC).

Grants and Fellowships: McKnight Foundation, Le Comte Du Nouy Foundation, The New York Foundation for the Arts, The National Endowment for the Arts, The Rockefeller Foundation.

This play is for Tzi Ma

I used to stay up every night
I'd be so all alone
In my hand my trusty pen
I'd work it to the bone
Ghostwriter, writer, writer...

that's what they call me by name
Ghostwriter, for fortune and for fame

I been writin' down these old stories now
for eighteen years or so
People are startin' to call me a genius
I gotta tell 'em—no, no, no
A ghostwriter, writer
Tell me what do you have to do
Ghostwriter, writer, writer, writer
To get your story through

— Garland Jeffries, *Ghostwriter*

IN PERPETUITY THROUGHOUT THE UNIVERSE
received its professional premiere on 10 May 1988 at
Center Stage, Baltimore, Stan Wojewodski, Jr., Artistic
Director, Peter W Culman, Managing Director. It was
directed by Stan Wojewodski, Jr. The set design was by
Christopher Barreca, the costume design was by Robert
Wojewodski, the lighting design was by Stephen
Strawbridge, the sound design was by Janet Kalas, the
dramaturg was Rick Davis, and the stage manager was
Meryl Lind Shaw. The cast was as follows:

LYLE VIAL	Arthur Hanket
DENNIS WU	Tzi Ma
CHRISTINE PENDERECKI	Carolyn McCormick
MARIA MONTAGE	Jennifer Harmon
BUSTER	Laura Innes
MR. AMPERSAND QWERTY	Troy Evans

This production was subsequently presented at the
Hudson Guild Theater on 19 June 1988, Geoffrey
Sherman, Producing Director.

AUTHOR'S ACKNOWLEDGMENTS

For support of and participation in workshops and readings of IN PERPETUITY THROUGHOUT THE UNIVERSE, thanks to:

Larry Sacharow and River Arts Repertory; Len Jenkin; Laura Innes, Julia Newton, Tzi Ma, Bram Lewis, Tom Cayler, Diane Venora, Deirdre O'Connell, Rocco Sisto, Ron Nakahara, Ernest Abuba, Brenda Wehle, Daniel Davis; Walter Schoen, Gary Gisselman, and Arizona Theater Company; Troy Evans, Belinda Casas, Lisa Wolpe, Margery Murray, Scott Coopwood; Geoffrey Sherman and the Hudson Guild Theater.

Special thanks to George Lane, Kip Gould, Stan Wojewodski, Peter Culman, and Del Risberg.

IN PERPETUITY THROUGHOUT THE UNIVERSE was commissioned by Center Stage.

CHARACTERS

DENNIS WU
CHRISTINE PENDERECKI
LYLE VIAL
MARIA MONTAGE
BUSTER
MR. AMPERSAND QWERTY

The actor who plays DENNIS *plays* TAI-TUNG TRANH.

The actor who plays MR. AMPERSAND QWERTY *plays* OSCAR RANG.

The actress who plays BUSTER *plays* MISS PETERSON *and* JOCULATRIX.

The actress who plays MARIA *plays* CLAIRE SILVER.

The play takes place very late at night, in a series of offices and rooms in Manhattan.

PART ONE

1. *(Isolated in light:* TAI-TUNG TRAHN. *Thirtyish, chicly tailored businessman.*

Discovered with his back to the audience, curled in a ball. With an effortless leap, he jumps gracefully and lightly up on a table, and turns to the audience.

He holds the backs of his hands up to the light, his fists clenched. He fans his fingers, first one hand, then the other. On the second he is wearing long, red-lacquered, Fu Manchu fingernails.

He does a series of tai-chi moves, fanning his hands through the air.

He turns his hands over.

His palms begin to bleed. Profusely.

Blackout, as)

2. *(A reading lamp is turned on by* LYLE.

He tears open an envelope. He holds the letter up to the light and reads.)

LYLE: "This letter has been sent to you from Surinam for good luck. It has been around the world nine times. You will receive good luck six days after getting this letter. Providing you do not break the chain. This is NO JOKE." *(making a note)* No joke in caps. *(reads)* "Your good luck will also come to you through the mail. Send copies of this letter to people you think need good luck.

Do not send money. Fate has no price. Do not keep this letter. It must leave your hand within 96 hours. An R.A.F. officer received $70,000 after he sent his letter out. Joe Elliot received $450,000, and lost it because he broke the chain. While in the Philippines, General Walsh broke the chain, and lost his life six days later. However, before his death, he did receive three quarters of a million dollars from a mysterious leper. Please send twenty copies of this letter to your friends and relations, and see what happens to you on the sixth day."

(Pause;

LYLE *turns the light off, as)*

3. *(A room.* DENNIS *turns on a lamp.*

DENNIS *and* CHRISTINE, *tossing unlit matches into a glass bowl.)*

DENNIS: *(Tossing a match)* Landlords.

CHRISTINE: Lawyers.

DENNIS: Bankers.

CHRISTINE: Real estate brokers.

DENNIS: Cab drivers.

CHRISTINE: Mimes.

DENNIS: Mimes?

CHRISTINE: You know. Mimes. *(She mimes.)*

DENNIS: Slowly for mimes. Chiropractors.

CHRISTINE: People who unwrap hard candies in the theatre.

DENNIS: Vanna White.

CHRISTINE: Madonna.

DENNIS: Garrison Keillor.

CHRISTINE: Mary Lou Retton.

DENNIS: Shirley MacLaine.

CHRISTINE: Andrew Lloyd Webber.

DENNIS: Doctor Ruth.

CHRISTINE: Pee Wee Herman.

DENNIS: Landlords.

CHRISTINE: We said that.

DENNIS: Worth repeating. Landlords.

CHRISTINE: Male gynecologists.

DENNIS: Immigration/naturalization clerks.

CHRISTINE: All petty bureaucrats, now and forever, world without end.

DENNIS: Amen.

(DENNIS *lights a match and tosses it into a bowl. The matches flare.)*

CHRISTINE: I love this list. This list is my favorite. People to kill after the revolution.

(They watch the flame.)

DENNIS: Mimes.

(He smiles.)

CHRISTINE: Always a promise for someone we hate.

(She turns the lamp off, as)

4. (LYLE *turns on a light. He is alone. He opens a letter and reads.)*

LYLE: "This chain comes to you from Venezuela. I myself forwarded it to you. But it is sent anonymously. Since this chain makes a tour of the world, you must make twenty copies of this letter and send it to your friends, relatives, and acquaintances. Send it anonymously. Do not put your name anywhere. In a few days, you will get a surprise. This is true even if you are not superstitious."

(Pause;

LYLE *turns the light off, as)*

5. *(A light is turned on.* BUSTER, MARIA, *and* CHRISTINE *in the Montage Agency. Very late.)*

MARIA: Your previous employers.

CHRISTINE: Brown and Scott.

MARIA: John Brown and Dred Scott.

CHRISTINE: Yes.

MARIA: Brown Do You Have A Restless Urge To Write Scott.

CHRISTINE: The original.

MARIA: The unsolicited of the world.

CHRISTINE: It was odious. Predatory.

MARIA: A complex and, for the client, financially exhausting fandango. Akin to dance lessons for lonely widows. Pyramid schemes. Door-to-door encyclopaedia sales in public housing projects where English is a second language.

BUSTER: Chain letters.

MARIA: The unsolicited of the world. I'm not scoffing. They paid the rent.

CHRISTINE: Self-delusion is always in season.

MARIA: A hardy perennial. What name?

CHRISTINE: Sorry?

BUSTER: Your nom de succor.

CHRISTINE: Ah. Albert Rutabaga.

(Lights change.

A light comes on in The Brown and Scott Agency.

CHRISTINE *moves to greet* OSCAR RANG, *a shy man with a bow tie and a mss.)*

OSCAR: Jazzy. Zesty. Exuberant. It's a romance. But not a bodice ripper. Ballsier than a bodice ripper. More masculine. Sort of a thriller romance comedy adventure spy grand-guignol roman-a-clef love story. About a shy podiatrist and a gorgeous double agent with beautiful feet. Based on a true story.

CHRISTINE: A true story.

OSCAR: Loosely. Loosely based.

CHRISTINE: You're a podiatrist, Mr. Rang.

OSCAR: Yes. Yes, I am.

CHRISTINE: I've had several podiatrists.

OSCAR: Some specialties must just attract a more creative type person.

CHRISTINE: That must be it. Proctologists.

OSCAR: No. No, I wouldn't think so. No sense of humor.

CHRISTINE: You breached security, Mr. Rang.

OSCAR: I was in the neighborhood. I had an appointment with Albert. Mr. Rutabaga.

CHRISTINE: You rushed reception. You hurtled down the hall. A loose cannon. There was no appointment. You never had one.

OSCAR: We've corresponded.

CHRISTINE: No.

OSCAR: Certainly. You're Mr. Rutabaga's assistant.

CHRISTINE: I am Mr. Rutabaga. Have been for lo these many years. Brown and Scott's Rutabaga. For purposes of continuity. Client confidence. Many, many of our clients have been writing their first novels with Brown and Scott for many, many years. They'd never entrust their life's work to a new reader.

OSCAR: I see. You are—?

CHRISTINE: Fourth-generation Rutabaga. Believe me, Mr. Rang, it makes no difference.

OSCAR: So you'll be editing my manuscript, Miss—?

CHRISTINE: Christine Penderecki.

OSCAR: Penderecki.

CHRISTINE: Vetting. We like to call it vetting.

OSCAR: I know the term from Le Carré.

CHRISTINE: Sexier.

OSCAR: What's the first step? Vetting?

CHRISTINE: Vetting the manuscript is the second step. The first step is always money. For a series of escalating fees, Brown and Scott will edit your manuscript, and supervise an unlimited number of rewrites. This in no way obligates Brown and Scott to represent or otherwise promote said manuscript, but if they choose to do so, the usual onerous terms apply.

OSCAR: Gosh. Um, Brown and Scott represent a number of famous authors—

CHRISTINE: That's the hook.

OSCAR: Hook?

CHRISTINE: Yes, they do.

OSCAR: Chewy McTavish. Bingo Merkin. Mr. Ampersand Qwerty.

CHRISTINE: I don't think so.

OSCAR: He wrote ZOG.

CHRISTINE: Never heard of him.

OSCAR: ZOG is a great, great book.

CHRISTINE: Got by me.

OSCAR: Does Mr. Brown ever represent someone like me?

CHRISTINE: A podiatrist?

OSCAR: No, that's not what I—someone like me—unpublished, new—

CHRISTINE: Unsolicited?

OSCAR: Unsolicited. Does Mr. Brown ever represent unsolicited authors?

CHRISTINE: It's been known to happen.

OSCAR: Yes. Yes, it has.

CHRISTINE: Known to.

OSCAR: Chewy McTavish.

CHRISTINE: So the story goes.

OSCAR: They were hijacked together. A men's room in Morocco.

CHRISTINE: So the story goes.

OSCAR: Perhaps Mr. Brown will represent my novel. When it's finished.

CHRISTINE: You never can tell. After the sixth or so draft, he always takes a look.

OSCAR: Sixth or so? Oh, gee. Do you really think it might need that much work?

CHRISTINE: Brown and Scott like to say books are never written. They're rewritten.

OSCAR: How true. How true.

CHRISTINE: Very wise men, Brown and Scott. They also like to say the client never writes just one check.

OSCAR: Money is no object, Miss Penderecki. I'm in this for the duration.

CHRISTINE: That's swell, Mr. Rang. Leave a check with Phyllis on your way out.

OSCAR: Thank you, Miss Penderecki. Thank you so much. I look forward to working with you.

(OSCAR *exits.*

Lights change.

CHRISTINE *returns to The Montage Agency, and* BUSTER *and* MARIA.)

CHRISTINE: No more mid-life crisis novels by housewives and businessmen. No more slim volumes of inspirational verse. No more Self-Help-How-To-Be-Your-Own-Best-Friend-Diet-Masturbation-And-Gardening Books. Why are we conducting this interview after midnight?

MARIA: No doubt Albert Rutabaga lives on after you.

CHRISTINE: No doubt.

(Pause)

MARIA: I represent a handful of writers—no, let's call them *authors*—authors with intermittent literary cachet and *People* magazine profile. Their names appear semi-regularly in boldface in the better gossip columns.

CHRISTINE: The hook.

MARIA: Hook?

CHRISTINE: For the unsolicited of the world. The hook. The flashing lure. The glisten.

MARIA: The glisten. Yes.

CHRISTINE: The slender between-you-and-me illusory chance that super-agent Maria Montage herself will represent my first novel, negotiating over power lunch six-figure deals for spinoffs and sequels in all forms now known or hereafter invented in perpetuity throughout the universe.

(Pause;

MARIA *moves to the window.)*

MARIA: I like the solace. The ambient hum. I like the preternatural hush of offices after business hours. The checkerboard of lit and unlit windows in the buildings across the airspace. We are tempted to speculate. We are tempted to discern patterns. Frame tales. Here a lonely cleaning lady. Here an after-hours word-processor, no doubt an aspiring something, a struggling artiste, word-processing not his chosen profession. Here a bankruptcy. An embezzlement. The consumption of a controlled substance. A dalliance between married members of the same sex. A woman in a fur bikini. And many, many lawyers. Of course. Four and twenty windows, and a lawyer's face in every one. This idle speculation, this discernment of shadows and fog, is what we do. What our writers do. After all.

(Pause. She turns from window.)

MARIA: I no longer deal with the unsolicited of the world. Unless they have their own publishing. Unless they are self-propelled. Those with a restless urge to write are on their own. No more nickle-dime rewrites. No more sniveling self-expression. Now all my clients pay up front in full for their delusions.

CHRISTINE: How can you give up unsolicited? Don't you have a condo in Carmel? Home in Majorca? Guatemalan maid?

MARIA: I have seen the light. My new clients deal in radical themes. Hold views mainstream publishers find—repugnant.

CHRISTINE: Ah. Vanity publishing.

MARIA: Who's to say? Their works sell well.

BUSTER: This is more than a market. It's a constituency.

MARIA: Part of my new roster. New look. New image for Montage. Along with my commercial—Buster, what's that quaint Yiddishism?

BUSTER: Schlockmeisters.

MARIA: Along with my schlockmeisters, I am collecting apostles of paranoia.

BUSTER: Conspiracy theorists.

MARIA: Of the left and right—but these days mostly right. Paranoia transcends politics. Becomes spiritual. All sorts of believers come to me. Translators of the arcane, the alchemical, the occult. And the odd billionaire whose slim volume of inspirational verse composed while ravaging a rain forest will be published on silk sheets and bound between the leather of an endangered species.

CHRISTINE: Magic.

BUSTER: Panic. Panic.

MARIA: The color of these true believers on the political spectrum does not interest me. Prose style is apolitical. And Montage sees the prose is polished.

CHRISTINE: That's the job.

MARIA: Yes.

CHRISTINE: Ghostwriter. Ghost writer.

BUSTER: Yes.

MARIA: A service. Rather more honest than the perpetual but expensive opiate paregoric you've been doling out to the ever-hopeful ever-pathetic at Brown and Scott.

(BUSTER *hands* CHRISTINE *a book.*)

BUSTER: Mr. Ampersand Qwerty.

CHRISTINE: I've heard the name.

MARIA: Mr. Ampersand Qwerty is one of the self-propelled. Mr. Ampersand Qwerty has no need of Random House.

(DENNIS *appears in a light in another room.*)

DENNIS: He has Snowstorm. Snowstorm. The publishing arm of Aryan Universe.

CHRISTINE: Aryan Universe?

DENNIS: An organization dedicated to insuring white supremacy throughout the galaxy.

CHRISTINE: Do you believe in inter-galactic contact?

DENNIS: Did she tell you about Mr. Ampersand Qwerty?

MARIA: Mr. Ampersand Qwerty's works sell well. Precise figures are unobtainable. They do not appear on best-seller lists or in chain bookstores. Mr. Ampersand Qwerty's face has never graced the cover of a national publication printed on glossy stock. Nor are his books to be found in libraries. With the exception of smaller municipalities in the Great Basin-Plateau area.

BUSTER: High desert. Semi-arid.

DENNIS: Mr. Ampersand Qwerty is the author, so to speak, of several speculative books detailing a series of interlocking global conspiracies. A precise geography of hate. A visceral cartography of paranoia. Mr. Ampersand Qwerty's last book—

BUSTER: ZOG, which you have before you—

CHRISTINE: *ZOG*—

DENNIS: *ZOG*—

BUSTER: Not a biography of the late much-loved king of Albania—

DENNIS: *ZOG* a is white Christian supremacist acronym for Zionist Occupation Government.

CHRISTINE: Zionist Occupation Government.

DENNIS: The one you pay your taxes to. In Washington D.C. F.Y.I.

CHRISTINE: F.Y.I.

DENNIS: For your information.

BUSTER: *ZOG* did particularly well in the Great Basin-Plateau area.

MARIA: I'm going to put the office on a nocturnal schedule.

CHRISTINE: I'm sorry? Nocturnal? Evening hours?

DENNIS: She mean graveyard?

BUSTER: As oppposed to diurnal.

MARIA: Midnight to dawn.

CHRISTINE: How unusual.

BUSTER: Some seasonal fluctuation. Keyed to sunrise.

DENNIS: I've lost my engagement book. My life is over anyway. What the fuck.

MARIA: I think it will put us more in touch with the paranoid impulses of the night.

CHRISTINE: It will me, I'm sure.

MARIA: I'm particularly interested in the universal ebb.

CHRISTINE: Ebb.

MARIA: Just before dawn. When the pulse—slumps.

CHRISTINE: I'm game.

BUSTER: Welcome to Montage, Miss Penderecki.

CHRISTINE: Ghostwriter. Who was Mr. Ampersand Qwerty's previous ghostwriter? For *ZOG*?

DENNIS: Lefkowitz.

BUSTER: Lefkowitz.

MARIA: Lefkowitz.

CHRISTINE: Lefkowitz. What happened to Lefkowitz?

(DENNIS disappears.)

MARIA: I don't know. We've lost touch.

BUSTER: We are awaiting Mr. Ampersand Qwerty's new material. As soon as he delivers it, you'll start writing.

(CHRISTINE gets up to leave.)

MARIA: You know one of my staff.

BUSTER: Dennis Wu.

CHRISTINE: Yes.

(Pause. MARIA smiles. CHRISTINE exits.)

MARIA: Where is Lyle?

BUSTER: Vetting *Geronimo.*

(As MARIA turns out the light,)

6. *(LYLE turns on a light. He is alone. He has an absolutely enormous manuscript before him.)*

LYLE: *Geronimo. (Beat)* Part One. *(Pause. LYLE turns out the light, as)*

7. *(The office. As always, very late. DENNIS and CHRISTINE are playing the Chinese drinking game.*

DENNIS *wins three rounds in a row.)*

DENNIS: Five. Ten. Drink. *(She drinks.)* Fifteen. Twenty. Drink. *(She drinks.)* Nothing. Five. *(She drinks.)*

CHRISTINE: Fuck you, Wu.

DENNIS: You'll get the hang of it.

(BUSTER *enters office, pushing a dim sum cart loaded with manuscripts.)*

DENNIS: Love your dim sum cart.

(BUSTER *hands him three manuscripts.)*

BUSTER: Dim sum du jour. Har gow. Shew my. Nor my gai.

DENNIS: Three is a comic number in English. Why is that? Americans always tell jokes in three parts. A priest, a minister and a rabbi. A Jew, a Chinese, and an Italian on an iceberg. A talking dog in a bar always has three things to say: "roof", "roof", and "Dimaggio, maybe?" Weird custom.

CHRISTINE: Tell a joke Chinese-style.

DENNIS: Chinese-style?

(DENNIS *tells an elaborate joke in Chinese. Long. With gestures.*

He finishes.)

CHRISTINE: I've heard that one.

DENNIS: You should have stopped me.

CHRISTINE: And I've heard it told better.

DENNIS: You tell it.

CHRISTINE: How's the punchline go again?

(DENNIS *repeats punchline.*

CHRISTINE *repeats entire joke in Chinese, with gestures, verbatim, perfectly.*

Beat. DENNIS, *stone-faced:)*

DENNIS: You're just not a funny person.

CHRISTINE: Fuck you, Wu.

*(*BUSTER, *in a light.)*

BUSTER: I've been with Montage since the beginning. Before the beginning. My career as Maria's major-domo has been a real eye-opener. I now believe many things I didn't even know about before.

*(*CHRISTINE *and* BUSTER *exit.* DENNIS *turns out the light, as)*

8. *(*LYLE *turns on a light. He is alone, working, halfway through the gargantuan* Geronimo *mss.)*

LYLE: *(Sings)* Oh, Lord, take me back
I wanna ride in Geronimo's Cadillac.

(Pause LYLE *sighs, turns off light, as)*

9. *(*DENNIS *turns on an office light.* CHRISTINE *enters, with a copy of* ZOG.)

DENNIS: Check out ZOG?

CHRISTINE: Dennis. Zionist Occupation Government. Is he serious?

DENNIS: So serious.

CHRISTINE: I thought this stuff went out of style. Years ago. Bad taste. Mouthful of ashes.

DENNIS: It's like Dracula. You have to drive a stake through its heart. On the anti-Semitic spectrum, Mr. Ampersand Qwerty is a moderate. Compared to the Christian Identity folks. Who believe Jews are, you know. Of the devil.

CHRISTINE: Offspring.

DENNIS: Spawn.

CHRISTINE: Dennis. How can you write this?

DENNIS: I'm not writing it. I'm ghostwriting it.

(Pause)

DENNIS: Besides, Lefkowitz did ZOG. And he didn't flinch. This stuff is marginal in America. Maria's clients are marginal.

CHRISTINE: I thought you said they were a constituency.

DENNIS: A marginal constituency.

(Pause)

CHRISTINE: Dennis. Did you tell Maria I was looking for a job?

DENNIS: No.

CHRISTINE: Then why did Buster call me?

(BUSTER in a light.)

BUSTER: Miss Penderecki.

CHRISTINE: Yes?

BUSTER: We understand Brown and Scott grow tiresome. We understand you shop around. We offer you surcease from unsolicited.

CHRISTINE: Paradise.

BUSTER: Are you interview receptive?

CHRISTINE: Sorry?

BUSTER: When can you come in?

CHRISTINE: Sorry?

BUSTER: Tonight.

CHRISTINE: What time?

BUSTER: Late.

CHRISTINE: How late?

BUSTER: Very late.

CHRISTINE: How late is very late?

BUSTER: After midnight.

CHRISTINE: After midnight.

BUSTER: Before dawn.

CHRISTINE: Why?

BUSTER: It's a science project.

(Pause)

CHRISTINE: You're joking.

BUSTER: Maria prefers.

CHRISTINE: Okay. Why not? Where?

BUSTER: At Montage. In the Flatiron. We're in the apex. Above the Tiger Balm Massage Parlor. It says "Never Closed—Always Open." In Korean neon.

CHRISTINE: Never closed—always open. I like that.

BUSTER: Redundant but not redundant. Never closed—always open. Korean neon koan.

(BUSTER disappears.)

DENNIS: Maria knows John Brown and Dred Scott. They have lunch.

CHRISTINE: She does. So then why did she ask me about them in my interview?

DENNIS: To see if you'd lie. To see if you'd tell the truth.

CHRISTINE: Never closed. Always open.

(CHRISTINE picks up ZOG.)

CHRISTINE: I can't wait to see Mr. Ampersand Qwerty's new manuscript. What vile conspiracy rears its godless head. I overheard two women in the ladies room discussing the low-frequency sound beam the Soviets are aiming at some city in the Midwest.

DENNIS: What's it do?

CHRISTINE: Makes everyone irritable. Depressed.

DENNIS: Why blame it on the Soviets? I'd be depressed if I lived in the Midwest.

CHRISTINE: A subliminal Russian rumble. Somewhere in South Dakota.

DENNIS: There are no cities in South Dakota.

CHRISTINE: It's a theory.

DENNIS: Everyone has a conspiracy theory.

CHRISTINE: I must take another look at ZOG. Take a look. Strange phrase. Take a look. Take. A. Look. *(Beat)* Always a promise for someone we hate.

(She turns out the lights as)

10. *(LYLE turns on a light. He is alone, seemingly, with the enormous* Geronimo *mss.)*

LYLE: Tony and Susan Geronimo. Charismatic pentacostalists. Listen to this. "Most nuns, and many priests, not to mention the vast majority of lay Catholics, are unaware of the Vatican conspiracy. They are unaware that the Vatican, the Red Whore of the Apocalypse, controls the global media, popular entertainment, and the worldwide trade in narcotics, arms, pornography, and white slavery. They are unaware that the Vatican's thrall extends over the Kremlin AND the White House."

(DENNIS appears.)

DENNIS: China?

LYLE: Not a dent.

DENNIS: Superior culture tells.

LYLE: Listen to this. "The Vatican sponsored and controlled the Bolshevik Revolution, bankrolled the Nazi rise to power, and engineered the Holocaust."

DENNIS: That's a taste-free assertion.

LYLE: Unbelievable. And I mean that in the pre-lapsarian sense of the word.

DENNIS: Is it well-written?

LYLE: Shaky prose style.

DENNIS: That's why they come to Montage.

LYLE: That's why. This is my favorite. "It is a well-known fact that the Vatican assassinated Lincoln."

DENNIS: I heard that in Hong Kong.

LYLE: That's the sort of place you'd hear something like that. Jacket blurb: "Irrefutably proves the Pope is the anti-Christ—Satan's representative on Earth."

(LYLE *hands mss. to* DENNIS *and disappears.*)

DENNIS: I can believe that. The guy wears a mumu.

(CHRISTINE *appears.* DENNIS *fondles* Geronimo.)

DENNIS: I get a warm, warm feeling from this. Vast sinister networks.

CHRISTINE: Dennis, were you ever Lefkowitz?

DENNIS: I've perused the material. I was interim Lefkowitz. I was Lefkowitz for a week. I did the last chapter of ZOG. I love Papist conspiracies.

(CHRISTINE *takes* Geronimo *mss. from him.*)

CHRISTINE: How many legions has the Pope?

DENNIS: Stalin.

CHRISTINE: Very good. Stalin.

DENNIS: Divisions. How many divisions has the Pope.

CHRISTINE: Legions is more romantic.

DENNIS: I wouldn't characterize Stalin as high romantic.

CHRISTINE: The hidden Stalin. The unknown Stalin. Stalin at home. A side of the man we don't usually see. Do you believe in inter-galactic contact?

DENNIS: Are you a resident alien?

(They kiss, passionately. MARIA *enters. She watches for a moment. Then:)*

MARIA: Christine. Dennis. Have you seen Lyle?

DENNIS: He was here.

MARIA: Has he brought in *Geronimo*?

DENNIS: Maria. Have you seen my book?

CHRISTINE: He left the manuscript.

MARIA: Give it me. No. What book?

DENNIS: My engagement book.

MARIA: No.

DENNIS: My life is over.

MARIA: Mine would be.

*(*MARIA *exits with* Geronimo *mss.)*

CHRISTINE: Oy.

*(*LYLE *appears.)*

LYLE: The best part of the Geronimo program is the Geronimo Foundation. The Geronimo Foundation buys babies. They intercept unwed mothers on the abortion clinic doorstep, and pay them big bucks to have the baby and give it to the Geronimos. Then the Geronimos put it up for adoption.

CHRISTINE: Meanwhile bombing the clinic.

LYLE: You can't prove that. Although they may inadvertently contribute to the climate of violence—

CHRISTINE: They'd never resort to violence itself.

DENNIS: Never.

CHRISTINE: Even to do the Lord's work.

LYLE: Well maybe the Lord's work.

CHRISTINE: What's the catch?

LYLE: The catch. Why should there be a catch?

CHRISTINE: There's always a catch.

LYLE: The catch is they never place the little suckers.
That's the catch.

CHRISTINE: The babies.

LYLE: Right. They never put 'em up for adoption. They
keep 'em. They put 'em in these baby camps. Fascist
incubators. They raise 'em up to become storm troopers
of the Lord.

CHRISTINE: Where is this baby camp?

LYLE: Somewhere in California.

CHRISTINE: Quite a conspiracy.

LYLE: Everyone has a conspiracy theory. How can you
explain the world without a conspiracy theory?

(LYLE *disappears*.)

CHRISTINE: You and Lyle. You're both as paranoid as
they are.

DENNIS: Everyone has a conspiracy theory.

CHRISTINE: I don't.

DENNIS: You should. How can you explain the world
without a conspiracy theory?

CHRISTINE: I can't. I don't.

(*Pause*)

CHRISTINE: How is your conspiracy theory different from their conspiracy theory?

DENNIS: They have guns. Machine guns. With silencers. Uzis.

CHRISTINE: Great names, though. Aryan Universe.

DENNIS: You have to admire the names.

CHRISTINE: Aryan Universe. Snowstorm. The Arm The Sword and The Handgun of the Lord.

DENNIS: Fortress America. Posse Comatose. The Church of Jesus Christ White Man.

CHRISTINE: Do you believe in inter-galactic contact?

DENNIS: Camaros of the Gods.

CHRISTINE: Camaros of the Gods.

DENNIS: No way.

CHRISTINE: I don't get you, Wu. You believe in fascist baby camps, but you don't believe in inter-galactic contact.

DENNIS: Oh, man.

CHRISTINE: We can still be friends.

DENNIS: Are we friends?

CHRISTINE: If we were, we could still be.

(They kiss. CHRISTINE *turns out light, as)*

11. *(*BUSTER *turns on a light. She is alone.)*

BUSTER: I'm not a true believer, but you can convince me with facts. Tone of voice. Sincerity. I know when someone's telling the truth.

(Pause)

BUSTER: I believe in automatic writing. I believe in out-of-body experiences. I believe anything and

everything about Tibetan lamas, no questions asked. I
believe Paul *is* dead. I believe in the white alligators in
the sewers of New York who cause the steam to rise
when they screw. I believe the assassination
conspiracies. I know the CIA killed Kennedy, the FBI
killed King, and the NYPD killed Malcolm X. I don't
know about Bobby, but I have my theories. I believe the
Jesuits killed John Paul I. I believe the Society of the
Deadly Palm touched Bruce Lee in a certain way, and
his blood sickened and he died three months later. Just
touched him. Like this. Dennis also told me about the
Chinese Mafia in Amsterdam who deal in diamonds
and rhinocerous horn.

(Pause)

BUSTER: I'm not sold on Maria's new clients. Yet. I don't
believe the KGB is the root of all evil. But then again,
who's to say? I certainly don't believe the Vatican is
secretly financing abortion clinics and encouraging
illegal immigration from non-white Catholic countries
so that White America will be overwhelmed by large
brown Catholic families. Some people do.

(Pause)

BUSTER: I know AIDS is a CIA experiment they were
running in Central Africa that got away from them. A
mutated strain. Zaire. Haiti. New York. San Francisco.

(Pause)

BUSTER: I believe in inter-galactic contact.

(She turns the light off as)

12. *(Lights come on in office.*

CHRISTINE *and* DENNIS *are playing the Chinese drinking
game.* LYLE *enters.)*

LYLE: You got it, you got it, no doubt about it. Huddle
and cling, huddle and cling. Which game is this?

DENNIS: Chinese drinking game.

LYLE: Who's winning?

CHRISTINE: He is.

LYLE: What are the rules?

CHRISTINE: He won't tell me. He says I'll pick it up as I go along.

(BUSTER *comes through with her dim sum cart, wearing a slouch hat.*)

BUSTER: Read 'em and weep. Fry your retinas on these.

CHRISTINE: Dash Hammett.

BUSTER: Ray Chandler. My middle name is Noir.

LYLE: What's your last name?

BUSTER: Not a chance. Today's catch.

(BUSTER *hands* LYLE *a large stack of manuscripts.*)

LYLE: Oh, for a short stack. My life is over.

CHRISTINE: So's his.

DENNIS: I've lost my engagement book.

LYLE: I guess you won't be going out anymore.

BUSTER: No more satin nights.

LYLE: No more balmy dawns.

BUSTER: That's all over now, baby blue.

LYLE: No more controlled substances.

BUSTER: No more wet sticky sex.

LYLE: No more civilized conversation in boites.

CHRISTINE: What's boites?

BUSTER: A life of silence. A life of contemplation. A life of home entertainment. VCR—R.I.P.

LYLE: Perhaps people will call.

BUSTER: They'll assume he's died. Wonder what happened to old Dee Dub? Haven't heard from him he must be dead.

LYLE: You're right. Speaking of dying. I was on the train coming down. Packed ass to forehead, as per usual. It's always rush hour on the IRT. Even after midnight. There was a woman standing in front of me. I was sitting. Attractive. Very attractive. Asian, Dennis, I don't mind telling you. Wearing very tight slacks. Lemon-colored slacks. Mid-twenties. Beautiful body. Beautiful. This luscious curve. Her belly. The inner thigh. There's something about that curve. Makes you ache. The way the belly curves, under. The tops of the legs. Ache. I had this urge. No. I was seized, yes, seized by desire. I'm sitting, she's standing, inches away. I can touch her crotch with my breath. I feel hot. Dazzled. I want to slide my hand in, ever so gently, my hand, slip it between her legs. Caress that curve. Slowly. In. Up. Obviously I didn't do it. I wouldn't be standing here telling you about it now. I'd be calling you from Riker's Island.

(Pause)

LYLE: I have these moments. Runaway impulse. Stroke a stranger. Shoplift. Turn the wheel at 75 into the center divider. Late night moments of derangement. She would have screamed. Rightly so. She would have called for help. Called the police. I meant no harm. It was a tender impulse. A bad moment. I sat there, looking at that curve, stop after stop after stop, in a cold sweat. Aching to touch her. Shaking. I put my hands under my legs. I didn't trust myself. And my desire, by then, all tangled up with "My God, what are you doing? What are you?" Finally, I got up and got off the train a stop early, careful not to brush against her. I would have done it. I had vertigo. I wanted. Wanted to go over. It became so clear to me. Transparent. All I had to do was slip my hand between her legs, caress this stranger for a moment, and my life would be over. My life as I know it. And I realized how you can throw your life away. Like that. In an instant.

(Silence)

DENNIS: This just happened?

LYLE: My life is a mystery to me.

(MARIA enters with a man in a bow tie.)

MARIA: This is my staff. One of our most valued clients. Mr. Ampersand Qwerty, author of *ZOG*. Dennis Wu.

DENNIS: How you doin'?

MR. AMPERSAND QWERTY: Mainland, Taipei, or Hong Kong?

DENNIS: Staten Island.

MR. AMPERSAND QWERTY: Of course, of course.

MARIA: Lyle Vial.

LYLE: Like a pill bottle.

MR. AMPERSAND QWERTY: Lyle Vial. You know Biff Liff?

MARIA: And this is Christine Penderecki.

MR. AMPERSAND QWERTY: Charmed. Astonished. Where is Mr. Lefkowitz?

MARIA: Working at home today.

MR. AMPERSAND QWERTY: Rumor has it Mr. Lefkowitz is no longer with us.

MARIA: Us?

MR. AMPERSAND QWERTY: You. Montage.

MARIA: Not at all.

MR. AMPERSAND QWERTY: Word on the street. Deal with it.

(Pause. LYLE *slips out, unnoticed.)*

MR. AMPERSAND QWERTY: You'll see that he gets the new material.

MARIA: I'll hand deliver it.

*(*MR. AMPERSAND QWERTY *gives* BUSTER *a thick file.)*

MR. AMPERSAND QWERTY: Lefkowitz did a super job on ZOG. Just stupendous. So long.

(He starts out.)

BUSTER: This way out, Mr. Ampersand Qwerty.

*(*BUSTER *shows* MR. AMPERSAND QWERTY *out.)*

CHRISTINE: He doesn't know.

MARIA: Don't be ridiculous.

CHRISTINE: If he finds out.

MARIA: He won't. You'll study the file. You'll cop the style. As Dennis would say.

DENNIS: Very good, Maria. Way to speak American.

MARIA: Thank you. Where's Lyle?

CHRISTINE: Lefkowitz did ZOG.

MARIA: Most of it. All but the last chapter. Dennis did that.

DENNIS: I did it perfect, man. If he only knew.

MARIA: My little joke.

CHRISTINE: Why Lefkowitz?

MARIA: Mr. Ampersand Qwerty requested him.

CHRISTINE: Lefkowitz. Isn't Lefkowitz a Jewish name?

MARIA: Of course.

CHRISTINE: I don't understand.

MARIA: Something about a challenge. A provocation. A deep-seated belief in their superiority. He must be the best, he said. Who knows? Besides, you don't really think Mr. Ampersand Qwerty believes all that, do you?

(Silence)

CHRISTINE: Why didn't he finish ZOG? Lefkowitz?

MARIA: Disappeared. Vanished without a trace. Nothing missing from his efficiency apartment. Every page in place. Very neat, Lefkowitz. One might say anal. We reported to the police. Sub rosa. I didn't see any point in telling the clients. I still don't.

(As the lights go out in the office)

13. *(A pool of light up on* LYLE. *He opens a letter and reads.)*

LYLE: "Constantine Dat received the chain in 1959. He asked his secretary to make twenty copies and then forgot about it. A few days later, he lost his job. While berserkly searching for a revolver with which to slaughter his boss, his foreman, a co-worker who owed him twenty dollars, and another he suspected of sleeping with his wife, along with several relatively innocent bystanders, he found the chain in his upper right-hand desk drawer. The next day he sent it out to twenty friends and relatives he had intended to gun down in the street like dogs. Five days later he got an even better job and threw the revolver away. For No Reason Should This Chain Be Broken. Remember, send no money. It really, really works."

*(*LYLE *turns the light out as)*

14. *(*CHRISTINE *turns on a light in her room.)*

CHRISTINE: It was just before dawn when I began vetting Mr. Ampersand Qwerty's material. The universal ebb. The time of night when you see things scuttle across the floor out of the corner of your eye. Mr. Ampersand Qwerty's manuscript concerned a conspiracy. Of course. Conspire. To breathe together. That would be my guess.

(She opens the file.)

CHRISTINE: He began with a note to Lefkowitz.

(MR. AMPERSAND QWERTY *appears in a light.)*

MR. AMPERSAND QWERTY: We think the pop-fic approach the right approach for this—campaign. The non-fiction novel. The novel as history. History, a novel. Reality/Fiction. America's ready for it. America's in the mood. A best-seller, Lefkowitz. *(Sings softly)* Movin' on up, movin' on up. *(Breaks off)* Begin with the following preface: Dear Reader. The imaginative and speculative inquiry. Fact or fiction. The boundaries blur. When the source is "deep." When a thoughtless footnote might mean the sudden death of an agent in a far-off cold country. Then the techniques of fiction serve the interests of truth. A paradox? Perhaps. The story I am about to tell you is full of paradoxes. Rest assured every word of this astonishing tale is true. Don't scoff. Turn the page. Be amazed.

(CHRISTINE turns the page.)

MR. AMPERSAND QWERTY: Here are the facts. Make it up, Lefkowitz, make it up. Don't forget to mention the Hmong. The mysterious deaths among the Hmong.

(MR. AMPERSAND QWERTY *vanishes.)*

CHRISTINE: Mr. Ampersand Qwerty's file was a jumble of pamphlets, charts, wire-tap transcripts, immigration statistics, notes scribbled on cocktail napkins. Held together by a malignant certainty. This certainty promised and suggested a narrative. As I read, I began to feel a certain minor genre of pulp fiction might be successfully resuscitated for Mr. Ampersand Qwerty's ends. I started to sketch out an improbable plot. Using

as my point of embarcation an alleged transcript of a
purported interview. (CHRISTINE *moves to a computer
terminal and switches it on; it gives off a green glow. She
begins to write.*

Silence

Ghostly electric guitar in the far distance.

CLAIRE SILVER (MARIA) *appears.*)

CLAIRE: Following the debacle in Southeast Asia, with
typical American naïveté, we welcomed the debris of
Indochina into our country. We not only embrace our
enemies after hostilities cease, we bare our necks and
hand them swords. Boat people. Opportunists. Double
agents. Triple agents. Parasites. Warlords and drug
dealers. Arms smugglers. With a big open-mouthed
kiss we sucked the virus into our body politic. The
analogy seems apt in this time of plague.

(TAI-TUNG TRANH *appears.*)

TAI-TUNG TRANH: Plagues and rumors of plagues.

CLAIRE: Thank you for seeing me, Mr. Tranh.

TAI-TUNG TRANH: It is brave of you to come, Mrs. Silver.

CLAIRE: Knowing what I know about you?

TAI-TUNG TRANH: If I were what you think I am. But
I'm not.

CLAIRE: I know who you are.

TAI-TUNG TRANH: A merchant.

CLAIRE: A gangster.

(Pause)

TAI-TUNG TRANH: Mrs. Claire Silver. A professional
conspiracy theorist. Tracing the strands of the web back
to the KGB spider. This bombing of a synagogue by a
PLO splinter group in Brussels. This assassination of a
Turkish consul and used car dealer in Los Angeles by

Armenian terrorists. This heart attack of a Bulgarian dissident in London. You bring these incidents together. You make sense of them. You discern patterns. You seek a mastermind.

CLAIRE: Something like that. You've read my book?

TAI-TUNG TRANH: Your theories are well known. America is an amazing country. The most arcane professions of my homeland seem humdrum here. I come from a family of astrologers. In America, you have astrology in your morning paper. What is your theory about Tai-Tung Tranh?

CLAIRE: You are a former colonel in the Army of the Republic of Viet Nam.

TAI-TUNG TRANH: Mrs. Silver. Please. Take a close look. How old am I?

CLAIRE: I don't know. I've never been able to make out Asian ages.

TAI-TUNG TRANH: I am thirty-one. Too young, Mrs. Silver. Too young to have been a colonel. Even in the last days. When they were drafting twelve-year-old boys. No teenage colonels, Mrs. Silver. Your sources have made a basic mistake. They have confused me with my father. An understandable error. We all look alike. Fathers and sons, I mean. My father was a colonel in the ARVN. After the war—a redolent phrase, don't you think?

CLAIRE: After the war. Yes.

TAI-TUNG TRANH: After the war. After the war, my father—the Colonel—came to this country. He was forced to start from scratch. He took a job as a waiter. His fellow officers became cooks, bus drivers, postmen. His oldest friend, a neurosurgeon—a janitor at a private school. My uncles, a philosopher and a cellist, now own a small hand laundry in Greenwich Village. And so on. After the war, people of all classes risked life and limb to come to this country, where they were welcomed according to the time-honored American principles of refuge. Principles which make this beautiful country unique in the history of the world.

CLAIRE: Are you being ironic?

TAI-TUNG TRANH: Not at all.

CLAIRE: Good. You have no right.

TAI-TUNG TRANH: America transcends irony, Mrs. Silver. General Ky himself sold liquor in southern California. The doorman at your health club was a warlord in the Mekong Delta.

CLAIRE: You have been spying on me.

TAI-TUNG TRANH: A fairly notorious fellow. Do not forget him at Christmas time.

CLAIRE: Are you threatening me, Mr. Tranh?

TAI-TUNG TRANH: I am a merchant. I sell fish sauce and condiments. Do you care for Vietnamese cuisine?

CLAIRE: You are the oriental crime czar of a new Indo-Chinese Mafia which traffics in arms, narcotics, prostitution, and aliens.

TAI-TUNG TRANH: Asian crime czar. Orientals are rugs.

CLAIRE: You deny it?

TAI-TUNG TRANH: Mrs. Silver. In Saigon, we had servants. Do you understand? Now we are Americans. I sell fish sauce and condiments. You have crowned me the king of this imaginary criminal conspiracy. I am not your spider. The web is only in your mind.

CLAIRE: Hmong.

TAI-TUNG TRANH: Mung?

CLAIRE: Hmong.

TAI-TUNG TRANH: Mung is a bean, Mrs. Silver.

CLAIRE: Hmong is a people, Mr. Tranh, as you well know. Hill people from Laos.

TAI-TUNG TRANH: I know nothing of Laos.

CLAIRE: They worked for the CIA during the war.

TAI-TUNG TRANH: So did your doorman. They ran smack together.

CLAIRE: Now you are being offensive.

TAI-TUNG TRANH: Everyone knows the CIA ran heroin during the war. Air America. Claire Chenault. KMT warlords. The Shan states. Fortunes were made.

CLAIRE: Rubbish. Communist propaganda.

TAI-TUNG TRANH: You believe your conspiracies, and I'll believe mine.

CLAIRE: There have been a rash of mysterious deaths among the Hmong. I have reason to believe you know what is killing the Hmong.

TAI-TUNG TRANH: One of my favorite American things is the B movie. You sound like a B movie, Mrs. Silver. I have reason to believe. Rash of mysterious deaths. I know nothing of the Hmong.

CLAIRE: I believe you are instrumental in causing those deaths.

TAI-TUNG TRANH: Now you are being offensive.

(He claps his hands. MISS PETERSON *(*BUSTER*) appears.)*

TAI-TUNG TRANH: Miss Peterson. Show Mrs. Silver out.

CLAIRE: I can find my own way. *(She exits.)*

TAI-TUNG TRANH: If you ever need fish sauce.

*(*MR. AMPERSAND QWERTY *appears in a light.)*

MR. AMPERSAND QWERTY: So the only interview on record with Mr. Tai-Tung Tranh came to an end. But so did Claire Silver's investigation.

(MR. AMPERSAND QWERTY *vanishes. Lights change. Sinister oriental movie music.* TAI-TUNG TRANH's *manner transforms from prosperous Asian-American businessman to malevolent inscrutability. He strikes a series of Peking Opera poses.*)

TAI-TUNG TRANH: The white devil knows too much.

(MISS PETERSON *has a pronounced Eastern European accent.*)

MISS PETERSON: You said it.

TAI-TUNG TRANH: She should never have mentioned the Hmong.

MISS PETERSON: Here is her file.

TAI-TUNG TRANH: Have you memorized it?

MISS PETERSON: At the Acolyte Academy we were taught to anticipate.

TAI-TUNG TRANH: You have the soul of a spy. I have read Mrs. Silver's chart. Her moon is in a malificent house.

MISS PETERSON: A pity.

TAI-TUNG TRANH: Take care of her.

MISS PETERSON: With pleasure.

(TAI-TUNG TRANH *vanishes.* MISS PETERSON *travels.* CLAIRE *appears.*)

CLAIRE: What do you want?

MISS PETERSON: May I come in?

CLAIRE: If you insist.

MISS PETERSON: I have come to betray my yellow master.

CLAIRE: Come in. Sit down. Won't you make yourself comfortable?

MISS PETERSON: Thank you. You are so kind.

(Miss Peterson removes her jacket.)

CLAIRE: There is a sudden smell of jasmine in the air.

MISS PETERSON: I am ready to tell you everything I know. Here is your file. You may find it of interest. He knows everything about you. Your family history. Your radical youth. Your real name. Your links to crypto-Fascist and proto-Fascist groups. Your frequent trips to the Great Basin-Plateau area. Your proclivities. Your liaison with a certain southern senator's wife. I've looked in your file. I've read deeply. I've exhausted you. I know everything. What you hate. What you dream. What you crave.

(She strokes CLAIRE's face.)

MISS PETERSON: I know what you want.

(MISS PETERSON turns out the light, as)

15. *(Lights cross-fade up to CHRISTINE asleep in her room at the computer terminal.*

LYLE *appears.*

The light in the room changes imperceptibly. A shadow falls across CHRISTINE. She awakens.)

CHRISTINE: *(Starting)* Ridiculous. Lyle?

LYLE: I let myself in.

CHRISTINE: Lyle. How did you get in?

LYLE: I let myself in.

(LYLE turns on a light.)

LYLE: I got this letter. It's interesting. Let's hear it.

(He unfolds a letter and reads.)

LYLE: "The Doomsday Book, the great survey of Norman England, undertaken by William the Conqueror in 1085, contains the clue. Doomsday, so-called by the common folk because there was no appeal from its authority, was a record of what everyone and anyone owned, and what it was worth. The Doomsday Book records the existence of one female jester. A joculatrix. Her name is lost. This person, this joculatrix, is the inventor of the chain letter. Her original letter was first circulated among the barons, and lesser nobles, and later the monasteries. It was lost and presumed destroyed during the Cromwellian Ascendency, but was later discovered, some decades after the Restoration, in a box at the Drury Lane Theatre during a performance of Sheridan's *Duenna*. It is this original chain letter, the first chain letter in the history of the world, which is being sent to you now. Do not break the chain. It is over nine hundred years old. Make twenty copies of this letter and send it to friends and acquaintances."

CHRISTINE: God, I can't wait. I'm damp all over. Let's hear it. The world's first chain letter.

(LYLE *searches the envelope; it's empty.*)

LYLE: Not here. Nada. Ah, a note. "Being mailed to you under separate cover."

CHRISTINE: Jeez. What a tease.

LYLE: The world's first chain letter.

CHRISTINE: The world's first comedienne.

LYLE: Norman standup. A riot. Sheep jokes.

CHRISTINE: I want to be a joculatrix when I grow up.

(*Pause*)

CHRISTINE: I fell asleep over Mr. Ampersand Qwerty's manuscript.

LYLE: It's getting dark.

CHRISTINE: Nasty stuff. White nightmare.

LYLE: I'm looking forward to receiving the world's first chain letter.

CHRISTINE: Speaking of nightmare. Have you heard of the Hmong? The mysterious deaths among the Hmong?

LYLE: How did you know I'd know?

CHRISTINE: You always know this sort of thing.

LYLE: Stone Age mountain tribesmen. Hill people. Laos. Poppy farmers. Worked for the CIA during the war. After the war—after the war, the gratitude of a grateful nation. We get 'em out of Laos so the communists don't turn 'em into spring rolls. Bring 'em over, put 'em down in the middle of ex ex cee America. San Francisco, city by the bay. Culture clash to the max. Hunting wildlife in Golden Gate Park, barbequed squirrel in peanut sauce, hot and sour sparrow, eating the neighbor's cats and dogs. The Hmong didn't savvy supermarkets. (Pause)

LYLE: The Hmong think they've been relocated to Hell. Noise, violence, crime. Rush hour on the Bay Bridge. The war seems peaceful by comparison. Cut off from their ancestors, no way to get back home from the land of the demons. Living in a nightmare world.

(Pause)

LYLE: The young men, twenty-five, thirty, start dying in their sleep. An epidemic. Healthy, no apparent causes. Just pop. Gone. Not a mark on 'em. The Hmong think it's ghosts. Demons.

CHRISTINE: What do the doctors think it is?

LYLE: The doctors. The doctors think it's homesickness. Cultural dislocation. A broken heart. Could be. But why just the young men? Maybe it's Agent Orange. Maybe it's yellow rain. CIA, KGB. But no apparent organic cause. And why just the young men? The doctors call it Sudden Unexplained Nightmare Death Syndrome.

(LYLE *smiles.*)

LYLE: The heart just stops in the middle of the night.

(He leaves.

CHRISTINE *goes to the computer terminal. The lights fade, leaving only the green glow of the monitor.*

Blackout)

16. (DENNIS *appears in a pool of light.)*

DENNIS: Camaros of the Gods. Boss chariots. Visitors from outer space are the architects of certain ancient civilizations. Mayas. Incas. Egyptians. Easter Island. Atlantis. Even the Chinese. Note the absence of Greeks, Romans, Phoenecians, and Hebrews. Note the implication inherent in this cosmic scheme. These little brown people could not have built pyramids and great walls on their own, lacking as they did Western technology. Therefore, they must have had help from a superior culture. And since white people were still living in caves, it must have been white people from outer space. Who came down in their Camaros of the Gods, and spread benevolence and civilization. White people from outer space. There are no black people in Star Wars.

(Pause)

DENNIS: Billy Dee Williams. Relax my hair. Is my hair relaxed?

(Pause)

DENNIS: The great American yearning for the extra-terrestrial solution. What does it mean? Can it be as childish as it seems?

(Pause)

DENNIS: I don't believe in inter-galactic contact. But I do believe in the international fascist underground.

(Blackout, as)

17. (CHRISTINE *turns on a lamp. She is alone in her room. Before her, a stack of books: ratty paperbacks, library books with plastic covers, a great variety.*

She reads the titles one by one.)

CHRISTINE: *Dr. Fu Manchu. President Dr. Fu Manchu. Emperor Dr. Fu Manchu. The Daughter of Dr. Fu Manchu. The Bride of Dr. Fu Manchu. The Shadow of Dr. Fu Manchu. The Drums of Dr. Fu Manchu. The Island of Dr. Fu Manchu. The Trail of Dr. Fu Manchu. The Insidious Dr. Fu Manchu. The Inscrutable Dr. Fu Manchu. The Wrath of Dr. Fu Manchu. The Mask of Dr. Fu Manchu. The Return of Dr. Fu Manchu.*

(She turns off the lamp, as)

18. (MR. AMPERSAND QWERTY *appears behind her. He turns on a lamp.)*

MR. AMPERSAND QWERTY: White nightmare.

CHRISTINE: Pop literature. Comic books. Movies. Tabloids.

MR. AMPERSAND QWERTY: Symptomatic. They reflect a genuine message. An authentic impulse we ignore at our own risk. The drugstore rack—

CHRISTINE: The airport newsstand—

MR. AMPERSAND QWERTY: The supermarket checkout counter. Thermometers, on which we can read the temperature of our latest fever dreams.

CHRISTINE: White nightmare. Who chooses? What's available. The inventory of fantasy.

MR. AMPERSAND QWERTY: We do. Or rather, they do. We think the popular fiction approach the right approach for this—campaign. No one ever went broke overestimating the vulgarity of the American public.

CHRISTINE: H.L. Mencken.

MR. AMPERSAND QWERTY: Very good, Miss Penderecki. The non-fiction novel. The novel as history. History, a novel. I call it Apocalyptic Propaganda. Prophetic Jeremiad. Reality/Fiction.

CHRISTINE: Reality slash fiction.

MR. AMPERSAND QWERTY: Reality slash fiction. Precisely.

CHRISTINE: Polemic. Insinuation, innuendo, rumor, hearsay, prejudice. It's—

MR. AMPERSAND QWERTY: Yes—

CHRISTINE: Rather—

MR. AMPERSAND QWERTY: Absolutely—

CHRISTINE: Lurid.

MR. AMPERSAND QWERTY: No question.

CHRISTINE: Intemperate.

MR. AMPERSAND QWERTY: Not sober.

CHRISTINE: Inflammatory. Incendiary. Racist.

MR. AMPERSAND QWERTY: We want something which will ignite the imagination. The popular imagination.

CHRISTINE: *Yellow Emperor: The New Dr. Fu Manchu.*

MR. AMPERSAND QWERTY: Brilliant, Miss Penderecki. Brilliant. Genius stroke. We knew you were the ghostwriter for us.

CHRISTINE: A fairy tale. Czar of new Indo-Chinese Mafia. Murder, drugs, gun-running. It's a potboiler.

MR. AMPERSAND QWERTY: And how brilliant of you to rescue the Yellow Peril from the trash heap of fiction fashion. A coup.

CHRISTINE: It'll never fly.

MR. AMPERSAND QWERTY: America's ready for it. America's in the mood. This is our task. Snowstorm's task. To awaken America to this new danger. Before we vanish as a civilization.

CHRISTINE: Yellow peril. Asian domination of the world. A yellow emperor.

MR. AMPERSAND QWERTY: Don't scoff. Turn the page.

CHRISTINE: Sorry?

MR. AMPERSAND QWERTY: That's our motto. Snowstorm's motto. Don't scoff. Turn the page.

CHRISTINE: If this Tai-Tung Tranh person exists, so what? What's one more American Mafia? It's an accessory. Comes with every new immigrant group.

MR. AMPERSAND QWERTY: The hook.

CHRISTINE: Hook?

MR. AMPERSAND QWERTY: How we get the attention of White America. Give them crime. Sex. Miscegenation. Appeal to the deepest recesses of their little hearts. The assumptions they hold but don't acknowledge. That Americans have white skin and round eyes. Everyone else is—marginal. Everyone else is here on our sufferance. Everyone else has a hyphen. The tribal instinct, far from being obliterated, has reached its purest expression in this century.

(Pause)

MR. AMPERSAND QWERTY: Don't scoff. Turn the page. There is another book. A serious study of global economics and demographics. Trends and projections. The economic aggression of Japan and the Four Tigers: Hong Kong, Singapore, Taiwan, Korea. The looming shadow of China. The sheer weight of billions and billions of people. Asian people.

(Pause)

MR. AMPERSAND QWERTY: The color of America is changing, Miss Penderecki. By the turn of the century, you won't recognize any major American city. It won't be English as a second language. English will be the second language. Your children will have to learn Spanish or Chinese to get a job. Snowstorm does not intend to let America become a second-rate power and a Third World country.

CHRISTINE: America assimilates. Everyone wants to be American.

MR. AMPERSAND QWERTY: Too late. Too late. Too late. *(Pause. MR. AMPERSAND QWERTY indicates CHRISTINE'S stack of books.)*

MR. AMPERSAND QWERTY: *The Mask of Dr. Fu Manchu. The Diabolical Dr. Fu Manchu. The Claw of Dr. Fu Manchu.* To this day they sell well in the Great Basin-Plateau area. Curiously, after the war, the author of these books switched tactics. Dr. Fu Manchu became our ally, fighting the greater evil of communism.

CHRISTINE: You sound skeptical.

MR. AMPERSAND QWERTY: Fu Manchu as a hero did not prove popular with the American public.

CHRISTINE: Who is Tai-Tung Tranh? Really.

MR. AMPERSAND QWERTY: A merchant.

CHRISTINE: Fish sauce.

MR. AMPERSAND QWERTY: Hardly.

CHRISTINE: And this other book? The true story?

MR. AMPERSAND QWERTY: We shall slip it into the interstices of our story. Between the inter-racial sex scenes. When will you finish? Did you mention the Hmong? The mysterious deaths among the Hmong?

CHRISTINE: How did you know?

MR. AMPERSAND QWERTY: What?

CHRISTINE: I was the ghostwriter.

MR. AMPERSAND QWERTY: We chose you. We thought you might be receptive to new forms.

CHRISTINE: All forms now known or hereafter invented. In perpetuity throughout the universe.

(Pause)

MR. AMPERSAND QWERTY: Contractual language. I never read contracts. My lawyers read them for me.

CHRISTINE: Wonderful phrase, isn't it? All forms now known or hereafter invented. In perpetuity throughout the universe. It's an attempt to buy a piece of the future. To protect oneself from the future.

MR. AMPERSAND QWERTY: The future is ours. If we protect ourselves.

(Pause)

CHRISTINE: What happened to Lefkowitz?

MR. AMPERSAND QWERTY: He disappeared.

CHRISTINE: I know that.

MR. AMPERSAND QWERTY: So do we.

(MR. AMPERSAND QWERTY *disappears.* CHRISTINE *turns out the light as)*

18A. (DENNIS *turns on a light in another room.* CHRISTINE *moves to him. They undress each other. They make love.*

The light gets very white, intense.

Sudden blackout.

End Part One.)

PART TWO

19. (CHRISTINE *turns on a lamp. She is alone, in front of the word processor. She switches on the monitor. It casts a green glow.*)

CHRISTINE: Just before dawn, I sat down to finish. I felt a queasy excitement. Illicit thrill. The Forbidden City. *Yellow Emperor: The New Dr. Fu Manchu.* I visualized the cover. A montage of faces. A handsome oriental gentleman. An attractive Caucasian woman. A flash of white breast. A ninja lurking in the background. I remembered my dream.

(*She begins writing. The green glow on her face intensifies, as the lights change. Chinese movie music, sinister, swells.* CHRISTINE *disappears.*

TAI-TUNG TRANH *appears, as he did in the opening scene. He uncurls his hands and turns the palms over. They are red and wet.*

MISS PETERSON *appears. Kneels before* TAI- TUNG TRANH. *Begins to wipe the blood off his hands.*)

MISS PETERSON: She bled profusely.

TAI-TUNG TRANH: She seemed—juiceless.

MISS PETERSON: She was the opposite of juiceless. She was—juicy.

TAI-TUNG TRANH: Succulent as bird-nest soup.

MISS PETERSON: Mmmmmmmm.

TAI-TUNG TRANH: You enjoyed.

MISS PETERSON: I enjoy my work. If I did not enjoy my work, I would do something else.

TAI-TUNG TRANH: Are you thinking of leaving me?

MISS PETERSON: Don't be paranoid.

TAI-TUNG TRANH: I would like that engraved on my cremation urn. "Don't be paranoid."

(MISS PETERSON *finishes wiping* TAI-TUNG TRANH'*s hands.*)

MISS PETERSON: I think I missed a spot. *(Licks it off.)* Yumsters. *(Smiles and rises.)*

TAI-TUNG TRANH: You would do anything for me.

MISS PETERSON: Don't be paranoid.

TAI-TUNG TRANH: Bring me the Master Plan.

MISS PETERSON: You mean?

TAI-TUNG TRANH: Yes.

MISS PETERSON: The Doomsday Book.

TAI-TUNG TRANH: I hate it when you refer to the Master Plan as the Doomsday Book. It is so melodramatic.

MISS PETERSON: I like melodrama. It keeps my interest at a fever pitch.

(She presses a button. A huge leather-bound volume appears.

TAI-TUNG TRANH *opens it.)*

MISS PETERSON: Shall I call the doctor?

TAI-TUNG TRANH: As I peruse the material. (MISS PETERSON *opens a wallet-sized Watchman, and presses in a number. A light appears reflected on her face.)*

MISS PETERSON: Doctor. Put that away. You're wanted in the War Room.

(She presses a button. The light goes out. TAI-TUNG TRANH *turns to the Master Plan.)*

TAI-TUNG TRANH: Ah, here is the heart of the matter. "The conflagration in Southeast Asia was the latest pearl in a string of carefully cultured stones that go back decades to the temporary defeat of Imperial Japan. There followed the victory of the so-called Communists in China, the Korean conflict, the French Indo-Chinese humiliation, and so on to the present day. The continued unrest in Cambodia, the openly capitalistic aspirations of Deng, the rumblings of rapprochement between Taipei and Beijing, the economic suzerainty of Japan and the Four Tigers, the Asian Diaspora in the West, all point to one thing. The colonization of America." Ah, Doctor. Come in.

(DR. OSCAR RANG *enters, and goes to* TAI-TUNG TRANH.)

TAI-TUNG TRANH: I was just browsing in the Master Plan. We seem to be on schedule. 1997 is not so far away.

OSCAR: No. No, it's not. 1997 is just around the corner.

(*He kneels before* TAI-TUNG TRANH, *and removes* TAI-TUNG TRANH's *slippers. He massages* TAI-TUNG TRANH's *feet.*)

TAI-TUNG TRANH: Where was I? "The colonization of America. Economic enthrallment." Ah. Ah. Ah. Yes. For an Occidental, your shiatsu is not bad.

OSCAR: Caucasian. Occidental is a college.

TAI-TUNG TRANH: Shut up. The master stroke of this scheme is the reversal of roles. Unlike the Mafia, who are essentially gangsters who dabble in business, we are businessmen who disguise ourselves as gangsters. Don't you think this is the master stroke? Miss Peterson?

MISS PETERSON: I think the master stroke of this scheme is its sheer unbelievability. It is paranoic.

(OSCAR *holds up a bottle of nail polish.*)

OSCAR: Mandarin red?

TAI-TUNG TRANH: Of course, Doctor.

(OSCAR *begins to paint* TAI-TUNG TRANH's *toenails.*)

TAI-TUNG TRANH: We will use the heroin money to restructure the global economy. By 1997, America will be a dependent. A satellite. A colony. You missed a spot.

MISS PETERSON: I hate it when you talk business.

TAI-TUNG TRANH: What would you like me to talk?

MISS PETERSON: Pleasure.

TAI-TUNG TRANH: Stay there. Come no closer. Let me describe your Caucasian features. Let me speculate on your favorite positions. Let me hear those sounds you make in anticipation. The low, throaty ones.

MISS PETERSON: That's not fair. You know what I like.

TAI-TUNG TRANH: Not everything. Surely you have not told me everything.

MISS PETERSON: Don't be paranoid.

TAI-TUNG TRANH: I find you inscrutable, Miss Peterson.

MISS PETERSON: As soon as you're dry, I will show you a secret.

(*She walks off, unbuttoning her blouse, and making low, throaty sounds. She turns and smiles. Music swells. She disappears.* OSCAR *finishes painting* TAI-TUNG TRANH's *nails.*)

TAI-TUNG TRANH: Now we have liquidated Claire Silver, the secret of the Hmong is safe.

OSCAR: Were the Hmong—

TAI-TUNG TRANH: Shut up. Don't interrupt. The Hmong are walking time bombs. The CIA used them as guinea pigs during the war. The Sudden Unexplained Nightmare Death Syndrome is the first manifestation of the plague the Hmong carry. We shall trigger an epidemic by means of a biochemical catalyst. At the same time conduct a disinformation campaign about its contagious qualities. The Americans will put the Hmong in concentration camps. Why not? It has happened before. They already hate the Hmong for their foreignness, their primitive ways, their *oriental* qualities.

OSCAR: Why do you want to martyr the Hmong?

(He fans TAI-TUNG TRANH's *toenails with a small oriental hand fan.)*

TAI-TUNG TRANH: It will blossom into a vast American reaction against Asia and the Asians in this country. Japan and China will be forced to close ranks to protect their financial investments, their nationals, their vast holdings. Asian-Americans will be forced to realize there is no such thing. They will never be American, no matter how many generations forget their language and their culture. Many will die, but you occidentals know how cheap life is to us.

OSCAR: It's so complicated.

TAI-TUNG TRANH: You are a mere podiatrist. How could you hope to understand? Believe me, the end result will be the economic suzerainty of the Far East. The twenty-first century belongs to us.

(He examines his nails.)

TAI-TUNG TRANH: A particularly subtle shade of mandarin. I commend your artistry. Now go away. I have something pressing. Miss Peterson may have started without me.

(Music. Lights change.

OSCAR *and* TAI-TUNG TRANH *disappear.*

Cross-fade to)

20. (CHRISTINE *at the terminal. Green glow.*

She finishes.

She pushes a number of buttons, and the manuscript begins printing out.

Slow light fade to)

21. (LYLE *turns on a light. He is alone.*)

LYLE: Two recent Japanese best sellers by Masami Uno assert Japan's current economic problems—the surging yen, declining exports—are the result of a conspiracy to "bash" Japan by international Jewish capital. These books assert Jews form a secret nation within the United States, where they control the major corporations: IBM, General Motors, Ford, Chrysler, Standard Oil, Exxon, AT&T. Quote, America is a Jewish nation, endquote. *(Beat)* Mr. Uno describes himself as a Christian fundamentalist. The titles of his books are *If You Can Understand Judea You Can Understand the World*, and *If You Can Understand Judea You Can Understand Japan*. *(Beat)* Mr. Uno's books have sold 700,000 copies. The first asserts the Jews caused the Great Depression, and are plotting another for 1990. The second asserts the scope of the Holocaust has been exaggerated. These books are popular with businessmen, and well-read among Bank of Japan officials. Other recent conspiracy best sellers in Japan include *The Jewish Plan For Conquest of the World* and *How To Read the Hidden Meaning of Jewish Protocol. The Secret of Jewish Power To Control The World*, published in 1984, was written by Eisaburo Saito, a member of Japan's upper house of parliament. *(Beat)* You think I make this stuff up? It's in *The New York Times*. I'll show you the microfilm. *(Beat)* Shichihei Yamamoto wrote a best-seller seventeen years ago called *The Japanese and The Jews*. It sold three million copies. Currently, there are 82 books in print in Japan with the word "Jew" in the title. An ongoing fascination.

Many books about Jews circulate old legends, including a persistent theory the Japanese people—or at least the Imperial family—are descended from the ten lost tribes of Israel. Some mention the historical persecution of the Jews and draw parallels with Japan, an island nation in a hostile world. Some promulgate the popular notion the Jews and Japanese were the principal victims of the Second World War. Some admiringly recycle bromides about Jewish financial acumen. One recent best seller is called *Make Money With Stocks Jews Aim At. (Beat)* Here's the best part. Mr. Yamamoto's book, *The Japanese and The Jews*, was written under a pseudonym. Isaiah Ben Dasan.

(LYLE *turns out light, as)*

22. *(Sound of printer. Lights up on*

DENNIS *and* CHRISTINE *doing one of their lists, tossing unlit matches into a glass bowl on each item.)*

DENNIS: *Attack of the Puppet People.*

CHRISTINE: *Attack of the Crab Monsters.*

DENNIS: *Attack of the Fifty-foot Woman.*

CHRISTINE: *They Saved Hitler's Brain.*

DENNIS: *Mars Needs Women.*

CHRISTINE: *High School Confidential.*

DENNIS: *How To Stuff A Wild Bikini.*

CHRISTINE: *It's A Bikini World.*

DENNIS: *This Island Earth.*

CHRISTINE: *Panic in the Year Zero.*

DENNIS: *The Fearless Vampire Killers.*

CHRISTINE: No, that's a good movie.

DENNIS: Come on. *Bring Me the Head of Alfredo Garcia.*

CHRISTINE: *Faster, Pussycat, Kill! Kill!*

DENNIS: I don't think Russ Meyer should count.

CHRISTINE: A genius of the jump cut.

DENNIS: Yeah sure, he's an auteur. No way.

CHRISTINE: *Sex Kittens Go To College.*

DENNIS: If you say so. *The House That Dripped Blood.*

CHRISTINE: *I Wake Up Screaming.*

DENNIS: *I Am A Fugitive From A Chain Gang.*

CHRISTINE: *I, The Jury.*

DENNIS: *I Married A Communist.*

CHRISTINE: *I Was A Communist For the FBI.*

DENNIS: *I Walked With A Zombie.*

CHRISTINE: *I Died A Thousand Times.*

DENNIS: *I Spit On Your Grave.*

CHRISTINE: A great, great film. What about porn titles? I love porn titles. They bespeak volumes about our subterranean selves.

DENNIS: They be speak?

CHRISTINE: *Back Door Santa. Wide World of Spurts. Pizza Boy—He Delivers. Lesbian Spies From Venus.*

DENNIS: You have to have seen these. You never saw *Lesbian Spies From Venus.*

CHRISTINE: I saw the ad. I saw the marquee. It's part of the zeitgeist.

DENNIS: Not on this list. *Yom Kippur Ninja Killers.*

CHRISTINE: No ninja, no kung fu.

DENNIS: Racist. How about those counterfeit documentaries like *Cannibal Holocaust?*

CHRISTINE: *Mondo Cane.*

DENNIS: Too mainstream.

CHRISTINE: Wait. This is a set. *Mondo Cane. Mondo Pazzo. Mondo Freudo.*

DENNIS: *Mondo Freudo?* Foul. You're kidding. I don't believe *Mondo Freudo* for a second.

CHRISTINE: You can look it up.

DENNIS: Casey Stengel.

CHRISTINE: Very good. I'd give a lot to see *Mondo Freudo* right now.

(DENNIS *lights a match and tosses it into the bowl; the matches flare.)*

CHRISTINE: I love this list. This list is my favorite.

(CHRISTINE *turns off the lamp.)*

23. (DENNIS *alone, in a light.*

DENNIS *tells the following joke in Chinese:)*

DENNIS: *Ney gee ng gee do* Cock Robin *mei yup ying yip gai gee chin hoy geo mut murn? Kurn jal hey geu jo* Penis Rabinowitz!

(The only English words we hear are "Cock Robin" and "Penis Rabinowitz."

Laughs uproariously.

Then tells joke in English:)

DENNIS: What was Cock Robin's name before he changed it to go into show business? Penis Rabinowitz.

(Stone-faced. Shrugs.)

DENNIS: His agent made him change it. See here, big guy. Penis. Penis. Penis. It's just—too—*ethnic.*

(Pause)

DENNIS: Names, agents, aliases, circles of self-delusion. It's an excellent joke for Montage. It's a venue-specific joke.

(Pause)

DENNIS: Translation is an illusion.

(DENNIS turns out the light.)

24. *(MARIA alone in a light. She wears a fur cap, fur coat, and sunglasses. She goes to the window.*

Pause;

MARIA opens her coat. She is wearing a fur bikini.)

MARIA: Wild thing. You make my heart sing. You make everything. Groovy. Wild thing. I think I love you. But I want to know for sure. Come on and move me.

(Pause. She growls.)

MARIA: Wild thing. You move me.

(Pause. She closes her coat.)

MARIA: One never knows what to believe.

(Pause. She turns out the light, as)

25. *(LYLE turns on a light. He is alone.)*

LYLE: Jihad. Holy war. Mujahedeen. The largest open air weapons market in the world is in Peshawar, Pakistan, on the Afghan border. Afghanistan is now the world's single largest source of heroin. And Pakistan has replaced Lebanon as the world's largest arms bazaar. Drugs and guns. Guns and drugs. In perpetuity throughout the universe. In the local lingo, heroin and arms are called Jihad Enterprises. Here's the best part. These black market arms, originally intended for the

Afghan rebels, are Soviet-made, purchased in the Third World by the CIA.

(He turns out the light, as)

26. (BUSTER *appears in a light.*)

BUSTER: I believe in crystals, harmonics, and pyramid power. I believe in the prophecies of Nostradamus. I believe birds are messenger entities from the etheric plane. I believe in the G spot. I believe Idi Amin is living in Saudi Arabia, in a mansion with four wives and a bowling alley. I believe he practices every day. I believe he is a deadly serious bowler. I believe he bowls with fervor. I believe I have seen a picture of him in his bowling outfit. White shoes, grey slacks, pink ball embedded with gold glitter, black bowling shirt with "Idi" embroidered in white over the left shirt pocket. I believe he has made inquiries about joining the American pro tour.

(Light fades out on BUSTER as sound of printer fades up.)

27. (DENNIS *turns on a light. He is alone. Sound of printer fades.*)

DENNIS: My life is a mystery to me.

(Pause)

DENNIS: I've lost my engagement book. I've missed appointments. Lunches. Trysts. Late-night rendezvous at the Half Ass Cafe in Chinatown. Authentic Chinese slash American cuisine. Pastrami on rice. Corned beef on rice. Ham and eggs on rice. *(Beat)* War, famine, revolution. The great displacements of peoples. The vast migrations of nations. The countless refugees. All part of a divine scheme. To create a greater diversity and higher quality of ethnic restaurants in New York City. God is a gourmet.

(Pause)

DENNIS: I came to this country when I was twelve. In the airport, we heard Kennedy had just been assassinated. My father was afraid they might send us back. Kennedy opened the door to Asian immigration. Raised the quota. My father opened a restaurant in the suburbs. Served white-style Chinese food. Chow mein. He cooks. The customers call him Pop. I became an American. Ran with the brothers. My father said, *Do ng gere doe bin gor jee hii nee do.* You live like a stranger in this house.

(Pause)

DENNIS: Wherever I go in the Chinese world, everyone knows I'm *mei kwok wah que*: An American. Tone of voice. Gestures. Way I walk. But in America, Americans ask me, what are you? What are you? You Japanese? You Chinese? What are you? *(Beat)* I was an actor. I went to an audition. They wanted someone to play a Cambodian refugee. This refugee comes to America. Finds a new life. They said, what are you? I said, American, what do you think? They said, no, what are you? Cambodian? No, Chinese. They said, we want a real Cambodian actor. I said, name two. Anyway, you can't tell the difference. I can't tell the difference. They said, the advisor on this project is Cambodian. He can tell. I said, Where is he? Let's see if he can tell. They said, you know, everyone wants to do this. I said, I don't. I left. I came to Montage. I became a ghostwriter.

(Pause)

DENNIS: I don't know. I don't know what I feel like. Marginal. Sometimes I think in English. Sometimes I think in Chinese. I count in Chinese.

(Pause)

DENNIS: Nowhere at home.

(He turns the light out, as)

28. (LYLE *is looking at the terminal screen. The green glow is the only light in the room.*

CHRISTINE *comes into the room. She starts.)*

CHRISTINE: Lyle. Goddamit. How did you get in?

LYLE: I let myself in.

CHRISTINE: I need to finish printing out.

LYLE: You need to go to remedial narrative.

CHRISTINE: It appeals to the feverish imagination. To the fecund and fevered imagination.

LYLE: It boggles the mind what some people believe.

CHRISTINE: This is a future best seller.

LYLE: No doubt. William Martinex was arrested when he tried to buy two fifty-cent lottery tickets with a counterfeit ten-dollar bill. He became a government informer. He penetrated The Silent Brotherhood, and his revelations resulted in the arrest and conviction of twenty-three of its members on racketeering charges. Murder, bank robbery, extortion, arson. Psychiatrists say arsonists suffer from low self-esteem.

CHRISTINE: What does this have to do with *Yellow Emperor*?

LYLE: I don't know. Maybe nothing. The Silent Brotherhood has links with the Klan, the Aryan Nation, and other neo-Nazi groups. They belong to Christian Identity, a church which asserts that Jews are descended from Satan. The race of Cain. The Silent Brotherhood issued a manifesto, declaring war on the United States Government because it had been taken over by the Jews.

CHRISTINE: ZOG.

LYLE: Well, here's the best part. According to the Federal indictment, the members of the Brotherhood were acting out the plot of a privately published novel called *The Turner Diaries*. In the novel, a racist state is established in the Pacific Northwest through terrorism.

(Pause)

CHRISTINE: A novel. So Mr. Ampersand Qwerty missed the boat with *ZOG*.

LYLE: Certainly not the primary source. Not the soul and inspiration. I'm sure they have *ZOG* on their bookshelves. Background theory.

CHRISTINE: So that's why he turned to fiction. To fiction that calls itself fiction.

LYLE: Mr. Ampersand Qwerty thinks *Yellow Emperor* will be a real force for change. A sort of anti-*Uncle Tom's Cabin* for the eighties or nineties. Whenever the next big recession hits. He'll release it at just the right moment. When the breadlines are being blamed on the balance of trade and the new Sino-Nippon consortium.

CHRISTINE: Snowstorm.

LYLE: Snowstorm.

CHRISTINE: White nightmare. What should I do?

LYLE: Collect your check. If you don't ghost it, somebody else will. Guess what I got.

(He pulls a large sheepskin page out of his coat and unfolds it.)

CHRISTINE: The world's first chain letter.

LYLE: Got it in the mail today.

CHRISTINE: Postage due?

LYLE: It was postmarked Asunción.

CHRISTINE: Paraguay. Garden spot of the Southern Hemisphere.

LYLE: I hear the Bavarian cooking is muy bueno.

CHRISTINE: What's it say?

LYLE: Dunno.

CHRISTINE: What do you mean?

LYLE: It's in another language.

CHRISTINE: Norman.

LYLE: Norman English, Norman French, what is that, Middle English? Not Shakespeare, thank you very much.

CHRISTINE: What are you going to do?

LYLE: Get it translated.

(Indicates monitor and MR. AMPERSAND QWERTY's *manuscript.)*

CHRISTINE: White nightmare.

LYLE: It's starting to get to me. *Geronimo.*

CHRISTINE: There's a sick thrill. Rings a primitive chord. Like looking at pictures of the death camps. You want to turn away. Avert your eyes. But you can't. It's not the pictures. It's not the images that make you sick, and close your eyes. It's the thing in you. The pulse in you that quickens. That thrills. You scare yourself. You close your eyes and turn your head. You deny the feeling. You still your heart. You'd like to have that moment back. That moment before you heard what you heard. Saw what you saw. But there they are. Images. Anecdotes. Half-remembered facts. Unfathomable statistics. I remember. I remember the first time I had that feeling. I was a kid. I was in the kitchen. The neighbor lady was telling my mother a story. Something she'd heard. Or read. Someone she knew, I'm not sure. About a woman. About what that woman did to her own child.

(Pause)

LYLE: Don't tell me.

CHRISTINE: You can imagine.

(Pause)

LYLE: No.

CHRISTINE: I had never imagined. A new world opened up before me. A world I had never imagined.

LYLE: Never the same. After.

CHRISTINE: No. It's the same feeling, though. All these years later. Reading his notes. Writing this story.

(Pause)

LYLE: I get chain letters every day. General interest chain letters. Special interest chain letters. Chain letters for blacks. Chain letters for women. Chain letters for Native Americans. Chain letters involving money. Chain letters involving photographs. Chain letters involving videotapes. Chain letters in Spanish. Chain letters in Urdu. Chain letters in Tagalog.

(LYLE *leaves.*

CHRISTINE *moves to the terminal and starts print-out again.*

Lights fade to)

29. *(A red room.* CHRISTINE *and* TAI-TUNG TRANH.*)*

CHRISTINE: Thank you for seeing me, Mr. Tranh.

TAI-TUNG TRANH: Not at all.

CHRISTINE: It's an ungodly hour.

TAI-TUNG TRANH: Yes.

(Pause)

CHRISTINE: Sorry. You look like someone I know.

TAI-TUNG TRANH: It happens. How did you find me?

CHRISTINE: I have a friend.

TAI-TUNG TRANH: I see.

CHRISTINE: He made inquiries at the King Sun Cafe.

TAI-TUNG TRANH: Ah, the Half Ass. You would like the Half Ass. Too bad women are not welcome.

CHRISTINE: How Old World.

TAI-TUNG TRANH: Old World, New World, Third World. How can I help you, Miss Penderecki?

CHRISTINE: I wanted a fact.

TAI-TUNG TRANH: Yes?

CHRISTINE: You are familiar with Mr. Ampersand Qwerty?

TAI-TUNG TRANH: Yes.

CHRISTINE: He claims you are a crime czar.

TAI-TUNG TRANH: A kingpin. A kingpin of the oriental underworld.

CHRISTINE: Yes.

TAI-TUNG TRANH: I love old movies. Old American gangster movies. Al Capone. Bugsy Siegel. Dutch Schultz. Perhaps Mr. Ampersand Qwerty loves them too.

CHRISTINE: Is it true?

TAI-TUNG TRANH: I shall sue him for slander when his book is printed.

CHRISTINE: You know about his book.

TAI-TUNG TRANH: Oh, yes. I am well-informed. He wishes to foment anti-Asian sentiment in this country. Tie it to economic difficulties. As they occur. Not a new idea.

CHRISTINE: Does it worry you?

TAI-TUNG TRANH: I have the utmost faith in the essential decency of my new country.

CHRISTINE: Are you being ironic?

TAI-TUNG TRANH: Not at all. I am a merchant. This is the greatest country on Earth. I am quite happy to be here.

CHRISTINE: And the shift in economic power to the Orient?

TAI-TUNG TRANH: America assimilates. That is its genius. And you, Miss Penderecki, what do you do? What is your interest in Mr. Ampersand Qwerty's book?

CHRISTINE: I'm the ghostwriter.

TAI-TUNG TRANH: Ah. America is an amazing country, Miss Penderecki. In my homeland, we have no ghostwriters. Only ghosts.

(CHRISTINE *smiles and leaves.*

Blackout)

30. (BUSTER, *in a light.*)

BUSTER: I believe D.B. Cooper is Idi Amin's bowling coach. I believe the body discovered in Brazil is not Josef Mengele, but Jimmy Hoffa. I believe SONY stands for Standard Oil of New York. I believe MIT stands for Made In Taiwan. I believe global economic collapse is imminent. I believe in the legalization of heroin. I got a postcard from Lefkowitz yesterday which assures me he is alive and well and living in Asuncion. I don't believe that. I believe Lefkowitz is disappeared. Has been disappeared.

(Blackout, as)

31. *(Printer fades out.*

DENNIS *turns on a light.* CHRISTINE *is there.)*

DENNIS: Wars create refugees. Who come to New York and open ethnic restaurants. It's a theory.

CHRISTINE: Sounds like NYPD to me.

DENNIS: NYPD? The boys in blue?

CHRISTINE: At last. A set of initials you don't know. New York Provincial Disease. A fever state characterized by the hallucination that New York is the center of the universe.

DENNIS: No way. No way New York is the center of the universe. Not enough Chinese. Hong Kong is the center of the universe. But wait until 1997. Try to hang on till then. Boom! 1997! Communists take over Hong Kong, boom! We all come to New York. *Then* New York will be *sang lun gor yu jal gair cheon sum!* The center of the fucking universe.

(Pause)

DENNIS: Let me read it.

CHRISTINE: Not yet.

DENNIS: *Yellow Emperor.*

CHRISTINE: *The New Dr. Fu Manchu.*

DENNIS: Modeled on anyone I know?

CHRISTINE: No.

DENNIS: I like to think I exert a powerful influence on all your waking and sleeping moments.

CHRISTINE: It was all there. I just wrote it up.

DENNIS: You named it.

(Pause)

CHRISTINE: You worked on ZOG.

DENNIS: That was different. That wasn't personal.

CHRISTINE: I could say the same.

(Pause)

DENNIS: You know me.

(Pause)

CHRISTINE: That's true. That disturbed me. Knowing you. Made it more—forbidden. That's what it is, isn't it? If it's not personal, it's an abstraction. Someone else's problem. *(Beat)* The limits of empathy.

DENNIS: ZOG. Nobody believes that stuff. Not anymore. The Nazi geeks at the Institute For Historical Review. But this anti-Asian shit. It's everywhere. *The Times Magazine* cover. Threat from Japan. Blood red rising sun. It's in the air. How we are putting America out of work. College quotas on Asian students. It's not our fault we're talented. Wake up and smell the coffee.

(Pause)

DENNIS: It's good to see the once-popular Yellow Peril coming back strong. I for one have missed it.

CHRISTINE: Boat people. The Domino Theory. Domino, domino.

DENNIS: Van Morrison.

CHRISTINE: Very good.

DENNIS: Don't call me yellow.

CHRISTINE: Ochre. Umber. Off-peach.

DENNIS: Tell the truth. Do I look yellow to you?

CHRISTINE: I'd have to see more.

DENNIS: Let me read it.

CHRISTINE: Not yet.

DENNIS: I'm anxious.

CHRISTINE: So'm I.

DENNIS: So my? That's Chinese for—

CHRISTINE: Shut up.

(They kiss.

They kiss again, more passionately.

Fades to black.

Cross sounds of printer coming up to)

32. *(LYLE turns on a light. He is alone.)*

LYLE: The Norman chain letter resists translation. Dennis says translation is an illusion. *(Beat)* Everyone has a conspiracy theory. A woman handed me a pamphlet on the subway. Written by a retired engineer in New Jersey. According to him, the superpowers hired this Tokyo think tank to devise a scenario for limited nuclear. Should it come to that. This scenario envisions the incineration of Shanghai, Tokyo, Dusseldorf, and Manila. In other words, according to the author, forty million dead orientals. Orientals in quotes. He includes Dusseldorf as an oriental city because it's inhabited by Prussians and Turks. I know, I know. Here's the best part. This think tank is sponsored by our quote oriental friends in Jerusalem. End quote. *(Beat)* I don't know what it means. But this shit is everywhere when you look. *(Beat)* Carlos has switched from the Palestinians to the Armenians. They blow up Turks. All over the world, even Dusseldorf. And he's financing his terrorist activities with smack. *(Beat)* I begin to see a pattern. Make the connections. That's the scary part. *(Beat)* A cab driver told me desertification is the result of a plot to manipulate the global weather. Starvation in the Third World is a consequence of this and other Western conspiracies, including contraception. Contraception, a double-bind genocidal plot. They buy it, their populations decline. They reject it, they have too many babies and starve. Heads we win, tails they lose. This cab driver was from Addis Ababa. *(Beat)* I ponder *Geronimo.* America will never be seriously anti-Catholic. Or even anti-Semitic. Echoes of the Old World. This is the New World. We have another Other. Other others. Who bear no resemblance. Creatures from another planet. Unmistakable in their foreignness. Aliens. *(Beat)* The Soviets have officially accused us of developing an ethnic bomb, a weapon which affects non-white populations exclusively. *(Beat)* I know they are working on anti- matter bombs. Laser X-ray bombs. Stroke bombs, which induce cerebral accidents in mass populations. Microwave weapons. Brain bombs, which affect mental functions through long wavelength radiation of great intensity. The Soviets are aiming one right now at some city in South Dakota. I forget which one. We're not doing anything about it. We're monitoring the results. *(Beat)* I think the human need for linear narrative, and narrative closure, coupled with our physiologically determined dualism which dictates our childishly Manichaean world-view—good guys, bad guys, Empire of Evil, Free World—plus our innate inability to tolerate the tensions of ambiguity, as a species, I mean, will bring on World War Three. We'll blow it up just to see how it ends.

(LYLE *turns off the light, as)*

33. *(A light goes on in The Montage Agency.*

CHRISTINE *is sitting across from* MARIA, MR. AMPERSAND QWERTY, *and* BUSTER.*)*

BUSTER: It's overdue.

MARIA: We are anxious. Anticipatory.

MR. AMPERSAND QWERTY: I've outlined your basic concept to Maria.

MARIA: Brilliant.

MR. AMPERSAND QWERTY: I'd go so far as to call it High Concept. Wouldn't you?

MARIA: I would.

BUSTER: Bookstores across the Great Basin-Plateau Area clamor. They yearn. They back order.

CHRISTINE: Finishing touches. Loose ends.

MARIA: Please have a Xerox on my desk in the morning. I don't like the idea of just one copy. What if something happened?

CHRISTINE: What could happen?

MR. AMPERSAND QWERTY: I'd like my notes back. When you're done.

CHRISTINE: When did you tell her you knew?

MR. AMPERSAND QWERTY: She told me.

MARIA: We had to tell him. That something happened, has happened to Lefkowitz. That you were Lefkowitz now.

CHRISTINE: What did you tell him?

MARIA: We don't know.

CHRISTINE: You don't know what you told him?

MARIA: We told him we don't know what happened to him.

(Pause)

CHRISTINE: What happened to Lefkowitz?

(Pause)

CHRISTINE: Let me rephrase the question. What the fuck happened to Lefkowitz?

(Pause)

CHRISTINE: He knows, Maria. He knew I was the ghostwriter from the beginning.

MR. AMPERSAND QWERTY: From the beginning? All right. Lefkowitz became fascinated by conspiracies. Working at Montage, you can imagine. A natural proclivity became an obsession. He began delving into the machinations of the world-wide heroin trade. An inexhaustible conspiracy. A life's work, unravelling. And who would believe the connections, the alliances, the depth of complicity?

CHRISTINE: Who indeed?

MR. AMPERSAND QWERTY: Any number of people could have disappeared him.

CHRISTINE: Disappeared him.

MR. AMPERSAND QWERTY: One of the newer verbs of the twentieth century. From the Spanish. Highly useful. Could have been anyone. KGB. CIA. ZOG.

CHRISTINE: One of his own? Wasn't Lefkowitz a trusted agent of the international Zionist-socialist-media-banking-homosexual conspiracy?

MR. AMPERSAND QWERTY: Don't scoff. Turn the page. I personally favor TTT as the agent of Lefkowitz' disappearance.

CHRISTINE: TTT?

MR. AMPERSAND QWERTY: Your friend, Mr. Tai-Tung Tranh.

CHRISTINE: You little devil. How did you know?

MR. AMPERSAND QWERTY: He called me himself. Wanted to know if you were my minion. I told him no, merely my ghost.

CHRISTINE: Local color. Background. Character detail.

MR. AMPERSAND QWERTY: That's what I told him.

CHRISTINE: He's quite obviously a merchant.

MR. AMPERSAND QWERTY: Indeed. He sells fish sauce and heroin. Wholesale.

(Pause)

CHRISTINE: The manuscript and notes are in a metal box in the freezer compartment of my refrigerator. They're quite safe. I'll have a final draft on your desk Friday night.

(Pause)

MARIA: Fine.

(CHRISTINE *gets up and exits.)*

MARIA: Buster.

(BUSTER *leaves the room.)*

MARIA: Do you know what happened to Lefkowitz?

MR. AMPERSAND QWERTY: Specifically? No.

MARIA: I don't believe you.

MR. AMPERSAND QWERTY: The truth exists independent of your beliefs.

(BUSTER *returns with a copy of the manuscript.)*

BUSTER: A good read. A page-turner from start to finish.

MARIA: The notes?

BUSTER: Couldn't get a copy of the notes.

MR. AMPERSAND QWERTY: It doesn't matter. I have copies of the notes. How soon?

MARIA: It's already proofed. Corrected galleys to you tomorrow night.

MR. AMPERSAND QWERTY: After that?

MARIA: Whenever you want. It's your publishing house.

MR. AMPERSAND QWERTY: Yes. Yes, it is. Isn't it?

(BUSTER *hands him the manuscript.*)

MR. AMPERSAND QWERTY: The fire next time. (*Beat*)
Snowstorm.

(*Blackout, as*)

34. (DENNIS *turns on a light. He is reading the finished
manuscript.*)

DENNIS: These people are aliens. Their agenda hasn't
changed since the Crusades. The perennial A-list. Jews,
blacks, infidels, gooks.

(CHRISTINE *comes into the room.*)

CHRISTINE: In perpetuity throughout the universe.

DENNIS: Aryan universe. Never closed, always open.

CHRISTINE: Aryan universe.

DENNIS: The dream of a pure white future. Snowstorm.

CHRISTINE: Star wars.

DENNIS: It's not great idea to let white people have
nukes.

CHRISTINE: We made 'em, we get to use 'em. Besides,
you all invented gunpowder.

DENNIS: True. We started the whole thing.

CHRISTINE: Then what happened? No follow through.

DENNIS: We got distracted by fireworks. What can I tell
you?

(DENNIS *puts manuscript down.*)

CHRISTINE: He said America's in the mood.

DENNIS: He knows what he's talking about. When did
he say that?

CHRISTINE: He paid me a visit. He knows I'm the
ghostwriter.

DENNIS: He knows about Lefkowitz.

CHRISTINE: He knows everything. He was at the meeting.

DENNIS: When do you have to turn in the manuscript?

CHRISTINE: I told Maria Friday night. *(Beat)* I saw Tai-Tung Tranh. He looks like you.

DENNIS: So?

CHRISTINE: He looks just like you. Everyone's starting to look alike. Mr. Ampersand Qwerty looks like a client from Brown and Scott. I think he's the same guy. He came there to check me out.

DENNIS: Don't be paranoid.

CHRISTINE: Little late for that.

DENNIS: What's he like? Tai-Tung Tranh?

CHRISTINE: A capitalist in a nice Italian suit. He believes in America.

DENNIS: Gotta be an immigrant. Lotta Vietnamese in Chinatown now.

CHRISTINE: Bother you?

DENNIS: No.

(LYLE appears.)

CHRISTINE: Lyle. Where did you come from?

LYLE: I let myself in. *(He sees the manuscript.)* Fini?

CHRISTINE: Si.

LYLE: The translation is giving me fits. It's not Norman. An obscure Gaelic dialect. Southern Manx. A dead language. They're running it through the computer now. Lends credence to the joculatrix theory. Once I get the computer translation, I'll do an adaptation. Something supple, clean, at once contemporary without being colloquial. Non-archaic. Translating from languages you don't know is not illusion, Dennis. It's art. Poetry.

(He picks up the manuscript.)

LYLE: Mr. Ampersand Qwerty is ecstatic. He loves it. *Yellow Emperor: The New Dr. Fu Manchu.* You did a brilliant piece of work for him.

CHRISTINE: He hasn't read it yet.

LYLE: They've all read it. Buster. Maria. I read it.

CHRISTINE: Where'd they get a copy?

LYLE: From you.

(Pause)

CHRISTINE: Can you get it back for me?

LYLE: No. But I'll tell you where it is.

CHRISTINE: Lyle.

LYLE: It's your baby.

CHRISTINE: Right.

LYLE: Buster's desk. Bottom drawer. You can jimmy it with a bobby pin.

DENNIS: No telling how many copies there are. Or where.

LYLE: He's on the warpath. Smells blood and the best-seller list. He can't believe he wasted all that time on marginal fanatic fringe shit like *ZOG.*

DENNIS: America's ready for it.

LYLE: America's in the mood.

DENNIS: This book is a carrier. It spreads plague.

LYLE: I don't disagree with you.

(Pause)

LYLE: I have to go turn in *Geronimo,* Part II. An illustrated history of the Illuminati. If I see any copies of *Yellow Emperor* lying around loose, I'll tuck 'em under my coat.

(He leaves.)

DENNIS: Snowstorm.

CHRISTINE: It's mine. I should deal with it.

(LYLE comes back.)

LYLE: Hear about Lefkowitz?

CHRISTINE: No.

LYLE: Found him chained to a pillar under the Manhattan Bridge. Off the coast of Chinatown. Positive identification from dental records. *(Pause)*

LYLE: Predictable.

CHRISTINE: How so?

DENNIS: He was doing a book on the scag trade.

LYLE: Some things are better left alone. Speaking of which, reading a fascinating new manuscript which scientifically proves that the body discovered in Brazil wasn't Mengele. It was Jimmy Hoffa.

DENNIS: Jimmy Hoffa hasn't been disappeared—he's just represented by William Morris.

CHRISTINE: Where's Mengele?

LYLE: Alive and well. Mengele will never die.

(LYLE exits.)

CHRISTINE: What's your position on D.B. Cooper?

DENNIS: Sounds like a list.

(He gets the bowl and matches.)

CHRISTINE: D.B. Cooper.

DENNIS: Jimmy Hoffa.

CHRISTINE: Robert Vesco.

DENNIS: Michael John Hand.

CHRISTINE: Carlos.

DENNIS: Abu Nidal.

CHRISTINE: Is this missing or most wanted?

DENNIS: What's the difference?

CHRISTINE: Martin Bormann.

DENNIS: Josef Mengele.

(As DENNIS *and* CHRISTINE *sow their list, lights cross-fade up on The Montage Agency.*

LYLE *is jimmying open* BUSTER's *desk.)*

CHRISTINE: Ambrose Bierce.

DENNIS: Amelia Earhart.

CHRISTINE: King Pleasure.

DENNIS: Who's King Pleasure?

CHRISTINE: A great jazz singer. Disappeared one day in the fifties. Made a couple of fabulous records. Believed he was born on Saturn, or something. Believed he was a baby planet nucleus.

*(*LYLE *pulls open the drawer. It's empty.)*

LYLE: Nada.

DENNIS: Hart Crane.

CHRISTINE: Weldon Kees.

*(*CHRISTINE *tosses a lit match into the bowl; it flares.*

An intense light erupts from the drawer, suddenly blinding LYLE. *He shields his eyes.)*

DENNIS: I love this list. This list is my favorite.

(Lights cross-fade to)

35. (LYLE *in a tight pool of light. Twilight country sounds.*)

LYLE: I've always had this sense of myself as a young aristocrat in the last days of Empire. A sense of waning. Walking through twilight. Dying light. Late summer. Rumours of trouble in the countryside. Green trees dark against a pure cobalt sky. Soft air. An insect hum. Fire on a distant mountain, burning through the night. Barbarian drums in the distance. An oscillation. Tremor. Hazy and shimmering. Aura. Seeing the aura. Hanging suspended. The unearthly quiet before the quake. The last still seconds of calm before the cataclysm.

(Beats of silence. A high-pitched hum, almost beyond hearing, growing in intensity, snapping. The light gets very white, intensifies. A flash and a horrendously loud slamming noise to black.

Then, the sound of a pennywhistle, as)

36. (*Light up on* JOCULATRIX (BUSTER) *dressed in bells and motley. She waves the original chain letter.*)

JOCULATRIX: This sheepskin comes to you from Whiffle-on-Trent. It has been around the country seven times. It has even been to Ireland. Make seven copies and send them to your friends and relations. If you are short of sheep you may use leather. Do not break the chain. Ethelrod the Alabaster broke the chain and became a leper, with hideous, awful, hot and cold running sores. Thomas the Confessor broke the chain and died three days later of blackwater fever. While in the Holy Land, General Walsh broke the chain and lost his life. Or his wife. One or the other. Sorry. I have these synaptic lapses. However, before his death, or hers, he did receive a quantity of gold finger-bells from a hydrophobic monk. Do not for any reason break the chain. This letter will bring you good luck even if you are not superstitious. You will be surprised.

(Pause)

JOCULATRIX: I believe in the valley of the Hunzas in Asia, where men live to be one hundred and five and father children, and women are beautiful and happy. I believe Saint Brendan sailed his leather curragh across the Western ocean and discovered a new world. It was cold, boring, crawling with brown-skinned cannibals, so he said, this must be Canada. I believe in Atlantis. I believe in the Seven Cities of Gold. I believe in the Fountain of Youth. I believe this charm will protect me from the fury of the Norsemen. Just kidding. I believe in inter-galactic contact.

(Blackout as)

37. *(A light is turned on by* DENNIS. CHRISTINE *comes into the room with several manuscripts.)*

CHRISTINE: Two copies, and the corrected galleys.

DENNIS: Lyle?

CHRISTINE: No sign of Lyle. Just as well. He's been at Montage a long time. He likes it there. I wouldn't want to see him get fucked up on my account.

(She goes into the other room.)

CHRISTINE: *(Off)* We'll cross our fingers. I've got the original notes. I think.

DENNIS: You think?

(She re-enters with a metal box.)

CHRISTINE: I think they're the original notes.

(DENNIS opens the box.)

DENNIS: It's cold.

(He opens it and takes out pages of notes and original printout.)

CHRISTINE: I'm conflicted about this.

DENNIS: I'm not.

CHRISTINE: You come from an authoritarian, patriarchical tradition.

DENNIS: Love knows no frontiers.

CHRISTINE: Who said that?

DENNIS: Stalin.

CHRISTINE: See? I told you he was a romantic.

DENNIS: Now you know what to get me for my birthday.

CHRISTINE: What?

DENNIS: A document shredder.

(He holds up the first page. She lights it.)

DENNIS: *Yellow Emperor: The New Dr. Fu Manchu.*

(He drops the flaming page into the bowl. He holds up a second page.

She lights it.

The lights fade.)

CHRISTINE: Always a promise for someone we hate.

(The lights fade out as they add pages to the flames.

The only light is the burning manuscript.

Blackout.

End of Play.)

FULL-LENGTH COMEDIES

COUNTRY COPS
Robert Lord
$4.95

GETTING ALONG FAMOUSLY
Michael Jacobs
$4.95

HIGHEST STANDARD OF LIVING
Keith Reddin
$4.95

HOUSE OF CORRECTION
Norman Lock
$4.95

THE REACTIVATED MAN
Curtis Zahn
$4.95

WHAT'S WRONG WITH THIS PICTURE?
Donald Margulies
$4.95

Shipping is $2.00 for the first book ordered, and 25 cents
for each book thereafter.

Prices subject to change.

WILD AND CRAZY PLAYS

full length, contemporary, & American

BATTERY
Daniel Therriault
$4.95

BEIRUT
Alan Bowne
$4.95

HARM'S WAY
Mac Wellman
$4.95

NATIVE SPEECH
Eric Overmyer
$4.95

ON THE VERGE
Eric Overmyer
$4.95

WALK THE DOG WILLIE
Robert Auletta
$4.95

Shipping is $2.00 for the first book ordered, and 25 cents for each book thereafter. Prices subject to change.

THE GREAT THEATERS OF AMERICA

PLAYS FROM CIRCLE REP
$12.95

ENSEMBLE STUDIO MARATHON '84
$4.95

SHORT PIECES FROM THE NEW DRAMATISTS
$4.95

**PLAYS FROM THE NEW YORK SHAKESPEARE
FESTIVAL**
$12.95

**HIGH ENERGY MUSICALS FROM THE OMAHA
MAGIC THEATER**
$9.95

PLAYS FROM PLAYWRIGHTS HORIZONS
$12.95

Shipping is $2.00 for the first book ordered, and 25 cents
for each book thereafter.

Prices subject to change.

A Life in the Theatre

OTHER WORKS BY DAVID MAMET
PUBLISHED BY GROVE PRESS

American Buffalo
Sexual Perversity in Chicago and *The Duck Variations*

A Life in the Theatre

A PLAY BY David Mamet

GROVE PRESS, INC./ NEW YORK

First Edition 1978
First Printing 1978
ISBN: 0-394-50158-6
Grove Press ISBN: 0-8021-0154-2
Library of Congress Catalog Card Number: 77-91884

First Evergreen Edition 1978
First Printing 1978
ISBN: 0-394-17040-7
Grove Press ISBN: 0-8021-4162-5
Library of Congress Catalog Card Number: 77-91884

Library of Congress Cataloging in Publication Data

Mamet, David.
    A life in the theatre.

    I. Title.
PS3563.A4345L5   812'.5'4   77-91884
ISBN 0-394-50158-6
ISBN 0-394-17040-7 pbk.

Manufactured in the United States of America

Distributed by Random House, Inc., New York

GROVE PRESS, INC., 196 West Houston Street, New York, N.Y. 10014

THIS PLAY IS DEDICATED TO
Gregory Mosher

We counterfeited once for your disport
Men's joy and sorrow; but our day has passed.
We pray you pardon all where we fell short—
Seeing we were your servants to this last.

Rudyard Kipling,
Actors

The Characters

ROBERT An older actor

JOHN A younger actor

The Scene

Various spots around a theatre.

The scenes in this play can be divided into onstage and backstage scenes. In the onstage scenes, we see JOHN and ROBERT portraying characters in various plays in the repertory theatre for which they work. A beautiful solution for staging *A Life in the Theatre* in a proscenium house was arrived at by Michael Merritt and Gregory Mosher, the play's first designer and director, respectively, in their production at the Goodman Theatre Stage Two, in Chicago. They decided that it might be provocative if a second curtain were installed upstage, behind which the audience for whom JOHN and ROBERT play their onstage scenes sits. This curtain is opened when JOHN and ROBERT work onstage, which is to say, playing in a play. Thus we see the actors' backs during their onstage scenes, and a full view of them during the backstage scenes—in effect, a true view from backstage.

A *Life in the Theatre* was first produced by the Theatre de Lys, New York City, and opened on October 20, 1977, with the following cast:

JOHN   Peter Evans

ROBERT   Ellis Rabb

STAGE MANAGER   Benjamin Hendrickson

The production was directed by Gerald Gutierrez; set by John Lee Beatty; lighting by Pat Collins.

The New York production of A *Life in the Theatre* included a silent character, the STAGE MANAGER.

Scene 1

Backstage, after a performance.

ROBERT: Goodnight, John.

JOHN: Goodnight.

ROBERT: I thought the bedroom scene tonight was brilliant.

JOHN: Did you?

ROBERT: Yes, I did. *(Pause.)* Didn't you think it went well?

JOHN *shrugs.*

ROBERT: Well, I thought it went brilliantly.

JOHN: Thank you.

ROBERT: I wouldn't tell you if it wasn't so.

   Pause.

JOHN: Thank you.

ROBERT: Not at all. I wouldn't say it if it weren't so.

JOHN: The show went well tonight.

ROBERT: I think it did.

JOHN: They were very bright.

ROBERT: Yes. They were.

JOHN: It was . . .

Pause.

ROBERT: What?

JOHN: An intelligent house. Didn't you feel?

ROBERT: I did.

JOHN: They were very attentive.

ROBERT: Yes. *(Pause.)* They were acute.

JOHN: Mmm.

ROBERT: Yes. *(Pause.)* They were discerning.

JOHN: I thought they were.

ROBERT: Perhaps they saw the show tonight *(pause)* on another level. Another, what? another . . . plane, eh? On another level of meaning. Do you know what I mean?

JOHN: I'm not sure I do.

ROBERT: A plane of meaning.

Pause.

JOHN: A plane.

ROBERT: Yes. I feel perhaps they saw a better show than the one we rehearsed.

JOHN: Mmm.

ROBERT: Yes. What are you doing tonight?

JOHN: What am I doing now?

ROBERT: Yes.

JOHN: Going out.

ROBERT: Mmm.

Pause.

JOHN: For dinner.

ROBERT: Yes.

JOHN: I'm famished.

ROBERT: Yes.

JOHN: I haven't had an appetite for several days.

ROBERT: Well, we've opened now.

JOHN: Yes. *(Pause.)* I'm hungry.

ROBERT: Good.

Pause.

JOHN: It almost makes me feel . . .

ROBERT: Go on.

JOHN: As if I'd earned the right . . . *(pause)* I was going to say "to eat," but I'm not sure that that is what I really meant.

ROBERT: What *did* you mean?

JOHN: A show like tonight's show . . .

ROBERT: Yes?

JOHN: Going out there . . .

ROBERT: Yes, go on.

JOHN: It makes me feel fulfilled.

ROBERT: Ah. *(Pause.)* Well, it can do that.

    Pause.

JOHN: I liked your scene.

ROBERT: You did.

JOHN: Yes.

ROBERT: Which scene?

JOHN: The courtroom.

ROBERT: You liked that?

JOHN: Yes.

ROBERT: I felt it was off tonight.

JOHN: You didn't.

ROBERT: Yes.

JOHN: It wasn't off to me.

ROBERT: Mmm.

JOHN: It did not seem off to me.

ROBERT: I felt that it was off.

JOHN: If you were off you didn't look it.

ROBERT: No?

JOHN: No.

ROBERT: Mmm.

JOHN: The *doctor* scene . . .

ROBERT: Yes?

JOHN: . . . may have been a trifle . . .

ROBERT: Yes?

JOHN: Well . . .

ROBERT: Say it. What? The doctor scene was what?

Pause.

JOHN: Brittle.

Pause.

ROBERT: You thought that it was brittle?

JOHN: Well, I could be wrong.

ROBERT: I trust your judgment.

JOHN: No, I could be wrong. I have been out-of-sorts . . . my eating habits haven't been . . . they've been a little . . . ♦

ROBERT: And you found it brittle, eh?

JOHN: Perhaps. I may have found it so.   A bit.

ROBERT: *Overly* brittle?

JOHN: No, not necessarily.

   Pause.

ROBERT: The whole scene?

JOHN: No, no. No. Not the whole scene, no.

ROBERT: What then?

JOHN: A part. A part of it, perhaps.

ROBERT: I wish that you would tell me if you found the whole scene so.

JOHN: It's only an opinion (of a portion of the scene)° and, in the last analysis, we're talking about a *word* . . .

   Pause.

ROBERT: Yes.

JOHN: I'm sorry if I sounded . . .

ROBERT: Not at all. I value your opinion.

JOHN: Yes. I know you do.

ROBERT: Young people in the theatre . . . tomorrow's leaders . . .

   Pause.

° Some portions of the dialogue appear in parentheses, which serve to mark a slight change of outlook on the part of the speaker—perhaps a momentary change to a more introspective regard.—D.M.

JOHN: Yes.

ROBERT: Both of us, or was it only me?

JOHN: Of course not. I told you that I thought *you* were superb. *(Pause.) She* was off.

ROBERT: You felt that too, eh?

JOHN: How could I not?

ROBERT: I know. You felt that, eh?

JOHN: I did.

ROBERT: Specifically tonight.

JOHN: Perhaps tonight especially.

ROBERT: Yes. *(Pause.)* Especially tonight.

JOHN: Yes.

ROBERT: Interesting. *(Pause.)* Yes.

JOHN: To me it's a marvel you can work with her at all. *(Pause.)* But to work with her so *well* . . .

ROBERT: You do the best you can.

JOHN: It's enviable.

ROBERT: The show goes on.

JOHN: I find much in that I must admire.

ROBERT: Well, thank you.

JOHN: Not at all.

Pause.

ROBERT: You have a job to do. You do it by your lights, you bring your expertise to bear, your sense of rightness ... fellow feelings ... etiquette ... professional procedure ... there are tools one brings to bear ... procedure.

JOHN: No, it's quite inspiring.

ROBERT: Thank you. *(Pause.)* The mugging is what gets me, eh?

JOHN: Mmm.

ROBERT: Stilted diction and the pregnant pauses I can live with.

JOHN: Yes.

ROBERT: The indicating and the mincing, these are fine, I can accept them.

JOHN: Yes.

ROBERT: But the mugging ...

JOHN: Yes.

ROBERT: It rots my heart to look at it.

JOHN: I know.

ROBERT: No soul ... no humanism.

JOHN: No.

ROBERT: No fellow-feeling.

JOHN: No.

ROBERT: I want to kill the cunt.

JOHN: Don't let it worry you.

ROBERT: It doesn't worry me. It just offends my sense of fitness.

JOHN: Mmm.

ROBERT: If I could do her in and be assured I'd get away with it, I'd do it with a clear and open heart.

Pause.

JOHN: Mmm.

ROBERT: That she should be allowed to live (not just to *live* . . . but to parade around a stage . . .)

JOHN: Yes.

ROBERT: And be *paid* for it . . .

JOHN: I totally agree with you.

ROBERT: She would make *anyone* look brittle.

JOHN: Mmm.

ROBERT: You bring me the man capable of looking flexible the moment that she (or those of her ilk) walk on stage.

JOHN: I can't.

ROBERT: No formal training.

JOHN: No.

ROBERT: No sense of right and wrong.

JOHN: She exploits the theatre.

ROBERT: She does.

JOHN: She capitalizes on her beauty.

Pause.

ROBERT: What beauty?

JOHN: Her attractiveness.

ROBERT: Yes.

JOHN: It isn't really beauty.

ROBERT: No.

JOHN: Beauty comes from within.

ROBERT: Yes, I feel it does.

JOHN: She trades on it.

ROBERT: She'll find out. *(Pause.)* Perhaps.

JOHN: It is a marvel you can work with her.

ROBERT: It's not a marvel, John, you learn. You learn control. *(Pause.)* Character. A sense of right from wrong.

JOHN: Yes.

Pause.

ROBERT: I tune her out.

JOHN: Mmm.

ROBERT: When we're on stage, she isn't there for me.

JOHN: Mmmm.

   Pause.

ROBERT: How'd you like the table scene?

JOHN: I loved it.

ROBERT: My, that scene was *fun* tonight.

JOHN: It looked it.

ROBERT: Oh, it was.

JOHN: I wanted to be up there with you.

ROBERT: *Did* you?

JOHN: Yes.

ROBERT: Where?

JOHN: Up there.

ROBERT: At the dinner table? *(Pause.)* You mean up there around the dinner table, or up upon the stage?

   Pause.

JOHN: In the house.

ROBERT: Around the dinner table?

JOHN: Yes.

ROBERT: Oh, yes, that scene was heaven. *(Pause.)* It made me glad to be alive.

JOHN: It showed.

ROBERT: The *audience* . . .

JOHN: Yes.

ROBERT: That scene was a little play. It was a *poem* tonight.

JOHN: Yes.

ROBERT: Just like a little *walnut.*

JOHN: Yes. (How do you mean?)

ROBERT: *You* know . . .

JOHN: No.

    Pause.

ROBERT: Well, I mean that it was *meaty* . . .

JOHN: Yes . . .

ROBERT: Uh, meaty on the *inside* . . .

JOHN: Yes?

ROBERT: And tight all round.

JOHN: Ah.

    Pause.

ROBERT: Now *that* is superior theatre.

JOHN: Yes. *(Pause.)* Mmm-hmm.

ROBERT: Where did you say you were off to?

JOHN: Now?

ROBERT: Yes.

JOHN: I was going for dinner.

ROBERT: Ah.

JOHN: I've been feeling like a lobster.

ROBERT: Ah.

JOHN: All day.

ROBERT: Mmm. Shellfish.

JOHN: Yes.

   Pause.

ROBERT: I can't eat at night.

JOHN: No.

ROBERT: No. My weight.

JOHN: You're having trouble with your weight?

ROBERT: Yes, always. It's a constant fight.

JOHN: But you're trim enough.

ROBERT: Do you think so?

JOHN: Yes.

ROBERT: Then that makes it worthwhile. *(Pause.)* Thank you.

JOHN: Not at all. What are you up to this evening?

ROBERT: Now, you mean?

JOHN: Yes.

ROBERT: I thought I might go home and read.

JOHN: Ah.

ROBERT: Perhaps take a walk.

JOHN: Ah.

> *Pause.*

ROBERT: Why'd you ask?

JOHN: No real reason.

ROBERT: Oh.

JOHN: Just asked. I'm just asking.

ROBERT: Well, *I* thought that I'd take a walk.

JOHN: Mmm.

ROBERT: Why did you ask me that?

JOHN: No real reason at all. *(Pause.)* Unless you'd like to join me for a snack?

ROBERT: A "snack." I really couldn't *eat* . . .

> *Pause.*

JOHN: Well, then, some coffee. I could use the company.

ROBERT: I'll walk with you a ways, then.

JOHN: All right.

ROBERT: Good.

> *Pause.*

JOHN: You have some makeup on your face.

ROBERT: Where?

JOHN: There. Behind your ear.

ROBERT: Yes?

JOHN: Here. I'll get it. I'll get you some tissue.

ROBERT: It's all right.

JOHN: No. Wait. We'll get it off.

> JOHN *goes after tissue;* ROBERT *stands on the stage.* HE does *vocal exercises.*

ROBERT: Did I get it on my coat?

JOHN: No. (HE *moistens tissue with his saliva and rubs it on* ROBERT's *face.*) There.

ROBERT: Did we get it off?

JOHN: Yes.

ROBERT: Good. I didn't get it on my coat?

JOHN: No.

ROBERT: Good. Good. Thank you.

JOHN: Not at all.

> *Pause.*

ROBERT: Shall we go?

JOHN: Yes.

> JOHN *casually tosses the crumpled tissue toward the trash receptacle Stage Right. It misses the container and falls on the floor.*

ROBERT: Mmm. One moment.

> ROBERT *crosses right, picks up the tissue, and deposits it in the appropriate receptacle.* All right. All gone. Let's go. *(Pause.)* Eh?

JOHN: Yes.

ROBERT: I'm famished.

JOHN: Me too.

ROBERT: Good.

> THEY *exit.*

Scene 2

ROBERT and JOHN *in the Wardrobe area.*

ROBERT: Your hat.

> *Pause.*

JOHN: Thank you.

ROBERT: Like an oven in here.

JOHN: Yes.

ROBERT: Got no space to *breathe.*

JOHN: No. *(Pause.)* Am I in your way?

ROBERT: No. Not at all. *(Pause.)* Quite the contrary.

JOHN *(handing* ROBERT *his hat):* Your hat.

ROBERT: I thank you. *(Pause.)* *(Soliloquizing)* My hat, my
hat, my hat. *(Pause.)* Eh?

JOHN: *Mmm.*

Scene 3

Onstage. JOHN *and* ROBERT *in the trenches, smoking the last fag.*

JOHN: They left him up there on the wire.

ROBERT: Calm down.

JOHN: Those bastards.

ROBERT: Yeah.

JOHN: My God. They stuck him on the wire and left him there for target practice.

ROBERT *(of cigarette)*: Gimme that.

JOHN: Those dirty, dirty bastards.

ROBERT: Yeah.

JOHN: My God.

ROBERT: Calm down.

JOHN: *He* had a home; *he* had a family. *(Pause.)* Just like them. *He* thought that he was going home. . . .

ROBERT: Relax, we'll all be going home.

JOHN: On the last day, Johnnie, on the *last day* . . .

ROBERT: That's the breaks, kid.

JOHN: Oh, my God, they're signin' it at noon. *(Pause.)* Poor Mahoney. Goes to raise the lousy flag, the Jerries cut him down like wheat . . . Johnnie, two more hours and we're going home. *(Pause.)* And those bastards went and cut him down.

Pause.

ROBERT: That's the breaks.

JOHN: No. Not by me. Uh-*uh.* Not by a long shot.

ROBERT: What are you doing?

JOHN *gets up and peers over the trench.*

What are you doing, Billy?

JOHN *starts over the top.*

JOHN: You hear me, Heinies? Huh? This is for Richard J. Mahoney, Corporal A.E.F., from Dawson, Oklahoma. *(Pause.)* Do you hear me? It's not over yet. Not by a *long* shot. Do you hear me, Huns?

JOHN *runs off right. A single shot is heard, then silence.* ROBERT *draws on his fag deeply, then stubs it out.* HE *uncocks his rifle.*

ROBERT: Well, looks like that's the end of it. . . .

Scene 4

ROBERT *and* JOHN *have just completed a curtain call for an Elizabethan piece.*

ROBERT: Say, keep your point up, will you?

JOHN: When?

ROBERT: When we're down left, eh, right before the head cut. You've been getting lower every night.

JOHN: I'm sorry.

ROBERT: That's all right. Just make sure that you're never in line with my face. I'll show you: Look:

ROBERT *begins to demonstrate the fencing combination.*

You *parry . . . parry . . . THRUST*, but, see, you're thrusting high . . . aaaand *head cut.*

May we try it one more time?

JOHN *nods.*

ROBERT: Good.

THEY *strike a pose and prepare to engage.* THEY *mime the routine as* ROBERT *speaks lines.*

And: "But *fly* my *liege* and *think* no *more* of me." Aaaaand *head cut.*

Eh? You're never in line with my face. We don't want any blood upon the stage.

ROBERT *knocks wood.*

JOHN: No.

Pause.

ROBERT: Please knock on wood.

Pause.

JOHN *knocks.*

Good. Thank you.

Scene 5

ROBERT and JOHN are in a Dance Room. JOHN is lounging, sweaty, after working out a bit. ROBERT is working at the barre.

ROBERT: Isn't it strange . . .

JOHN: Yes?

ROBERT: That people will spend time and money on their face and body . . .

JOHN: Mmm?

ROBERT: On smells, textures and appearances . . .

JOHN: Uh huh.

ROBERT: And yet are content to sound like shopgirls and sheepherders.

JOHN: Ummm.

Pause.

ROBERT: It's quite as important as physical beauty.

JOHN: On the stage, you mean.

ROBERT: On the stage and otherwise.

JOHN: Mmm.

ROBERT: *Sound.*

JOHN: Yes.

ROBERT: The crown prince of phenomena.

JOHN: Quite.

ROBERT: An ugly sound, to me, is more offensive than an ugly odor.

JOHN: Really?

ROBERT: Yes. To me, an ugly *sound* is an extension of an ugly soul. An indice of lacking aesthetic. *(Pause.)* I don't like them. I don't like ugly sounds. I don't like the folks that make them. *(Pause.)* You think that's harsh, don't you?

JOHN: Not at all.

ROBERT: You don't?

JOHN: No.

ROBERT: I know. I'm strange about this. It's a peeve of mine. To me it's like an odor. Sound. For it emanates from within. *(Pause.)* Sound and odor germinate within, and are *perceived* within. *(Pause.)* You see?

JOHN: No.

Pause.

ROBERT: All that I am saying is that it comes from within. *(Pause.)* Sound comes from within. You see?

JOHN: Mmmm.

ROBERT: I am not opposed to odors. *(Pause.)* On principle.

JOHN: No.

Pause.

ROBERT: Do you know when I was young my voice was very raspy.

JOHN: No.

ROBERT: But I was .vain, I was untaught. I felt my vocal quality—a defect, in effect—was a positive attribute, a contributory portion of my style.

JOHN: Mmm.

ROBERT: What is style?

JOHN: What?

ROBERT: Style is *nothing.*

JOHN: No?

ROBERT: Style is a paper bag. Its only shape comes from its contents. *(Pause.)* However, I was young. I made a fetish of my imperfections.

JOHN: It's a common fault.

ROBERT: It makes me blush today to think about it.

Pause.

JOHN: Don't think about it.

Pause.

ROBERT: You're right. You start from the beginning and go through the middle and wind up at the end.

JOHN: Yes.

Pause.

ROBERT: A little like a play. Keep your back straight.

JOHN: Mmm.

ROBERT: We must not be afraid of process.

JOHN: No.

ROBERT: We must not lie about our antecedents.

JOHN: No.

ROBERT: We must not be second-class citizens. *(Pause.)* We must not be clowns whose sole desire is to please. We have a right to learn.

Pause.

JOHN: Is my back straight?

ROBERT: No. *(Pause.)* Do you *follow* me?

JOHN: I think I do.

ROBERT: We must not be afraid to *grow*. We must support each other, John. This is the wondrous thing *about* the theatre, this potential.

JOHN: Mmmm.

ROBERT: Our history goes back as far as Man's. Our aspirations in the Theatre are much the *same* as man's. *(Pause.)* (Don't you think?)

JOHN: Yes.

Pause.

ROBERT: We *are* society. Keep your back straight, John. The mirror is your friend. *(Pause.)* For a few more years. *(Pause.)* What have we to fear, John, from *phenomena? (Pause.)* We are explorers of the *soul.*

Pause.

JOHN: Is my back straight?

ROBERT: No.

Scene 6

The end of a day. JOHN *is on the backstage telephone.*

JOHN: Oh, no. I can't. I'm going out with someone in the show. *(Pause.)* No, in fact, an *Actor.* *(Pause.)* I don't know . . . Midnight. *(Pause.)* I'd like that very much. *(Pause.)* Me, too. *(Pause.)* How have you been?

ROBERT *enters.*

ROBERT: You ready?

JOHN *(covering phone):* Yes. *(into phone)* I'll see you then. *(Pause.)* 'Bye.

HE *hangs up telephone.*

ROBERT: We all must have an outside life, John. This is an essential.

JOHN: Yes.

ROBERT: Who was it?

Pause.

JOHN: A friend.

Scene 7

A short scene in which JOHN *and* ROBERT *encounter each other coming into the theatre for an early-morning rehearsal.*

ROBERT: Good morning.

JOHN: Morning.

ROBERT: 'Nother day, eh?

JOHN: Yes.

ROBERT: Another day. (HE *sighs.*) Another day.

Scene 8

Before a performance—at the makeup table.

JOHN: May I have the tissue, please? Thank you. How do you feel this evening?

ROBERT: Tight. I feel a little tight. It's going to be a vibrant show tonight. I feel coiled up.

JOHN: Mmm.

ROBERT: But I don't feel tense.

JOHN: No?

ROBERT: No. Never feel tense. I almost never feel tense on stage. I feel ready to act. That's a lovely brush.

JOHN: This?

ROBERT: No. The quarter-inch.

JOHN: This one?

ROBERT: Yes. Is it new?

JOHN: It's an eighth-inch.

ROBERT: That one?

JOHN: Yes.

ROBERT: That's an eighth-inch?

JOHN: Yes.

   Pause.

ROBERT: Well, it's awfully splayed, don't you think?

JOHN: No.

ROBERT: It's not splayed a bit?

JOHN: No.

ROBERT: Well, it's not *new* . . . (Is it new?)

JOHN: No, I've had it a while.

ROBERT: A while, eh?

JOHN: Yes.

ROBERT: A long while?

JOHN: Yes.

ROBERT: What is it, camel?

JOHN: It's sable.

   Pause.

ROBERT: (Sable brushes.) You keep your things well.

JOHN: Mmm.

ROBERT: It's impressive. No. It's one of the things which
   impressed me first about you.

JOHN: Mmm.

ROBERT: You take excellent care of your tools. *(Pause.)* May I ask you something, John?

JOHN: Of course.

ROBERT: Could you do me a favor?

JOHN: What?

Pause.

ROBERT: In our scene tonight . . .

JOHN: Yes?

ROBERT: Mmmm . . .

JOHN: What?

ROBERT: Could you . . . perhaps . . . *do* less?

JOHN: *Do* less?

ROBERT: Yes.

JOHN: *Do* less???

ROBERT: Yes . . .

Pause.

JOHN: Do less *what???*

ROBERT: You know.

JOHN: You mean . . . what do you mean?

Pause.

ROBERT: You know.

JOHN: Do you mean I'm walking on your scene? *(Pause.)* What do you mean?

ROBERT: Nothing. It's a thought I had. An aesthetic consideration.

JOHN: Mmm.

ROBERT: I thought maybe if you *did* less . . .

JOHN: Yes?

ROBERT: *You* know.

JOHN: If I *did* less.

ROBERT: Yes.

JOHN: Well, thank you for the thought.

ROBERT: I don't think you have to be like that.

JOHN: I'm sorry.

ROBERT: Are you?

JOHN: I accept the comment in the spirit in which it was, I am sure, intended.

   Pause.

ROBERT: It *was* intended in that spirit, John.

JOHN: I know it was.

ROBERT: How could it be intended otherwise?

JOHN: It couldn't.

ROBERT: Well, you *know* it couldn't.

JOHN: Yes, I know.

ROBERT: It hurts me when you take it personally. (HE *stands.*) Shit!

JOHN: What?

ROBERT: My zipper's broken.

JOHN: Do you want a safety pin?

ROBERT: I have one.

JOHN *(rising, starting to leave):* Do you want me to send the woman in?

ROBERT: No. No. I'll manage. Shit. Oh, shit.

JOHN: You're sure?

ROBERT: Yes.

JOHN: You don't want the woman?

ROBERT: No. I do not want the woman. Thank you.

JOHN: You want me to pin it for you?

ROBERT: No.

JOHN: I'll do it. Let me pin it for you.

ROBERT: No. Thank you. No. I'll get it.

JOHN: Oh, come on. I'll do it. Come on.

   JOHN *pulls out chair.*

   Get up here. Come on. Get up.

ROBERT *gets up on the chair.* Give me the pin. Come on.

ROBERT *hands* JOHN *the pin.* JOHN *drops it on the floor.*

Shit.

JOHN *gets down on hands and knees to look for it.*

ROBERT: Oh, Christ.

JOHN: You got another one?

ROBERT: No. Oh, Christ, come on. Come on.

JOHN: I'm *looking* for it, for God's sake.

ROBERT: There!

JOHN: Stand still now.

ROBERT: Come on, come on.

JOHN *attempts to pin* ROBERT*'s fly.*

Put it in.

JOHN: Just hold still for a moment.

ROBERT: Come *on,* for God's sake!

JOHN: All right. All right. You know, I think you're gaining weight . . .

ROBERT: Oh, fuck you. Will you stick it in?

JOHN: Hold still. There.

Pause.

JOHN: No.

Pause.

ROBERT: She's told you that I am the father.

JOHN: Yes. *(Pause.)* What are we going to do about this?

ROBERT: I don't know, David. You could—I suppose you could do me some physical damage. . . .

JOHN: Yes.

ROBERT: Or we could sit and discuss this as gentlemen. Which would you prefer?

JOHN: Which, in the end, is more civilized, John?

ROBERT: I don't know, David, I don't know. *(Long pause . . . intercom rings)* I asked you to hold all calls. *(Pause.)* Perhaps *you* should take this.

Scene 10

Backstage in the Wardrobe area.

ROBERT: The motherfucking leeches. The sots. *(Pause.)* The bloody boors. All of them . . . All of them . . .

JOHN: Who?

ROBERT: All of them.

JOHN: All of whom?

Pause.

ROBERT: What?

JOHN: All of whom?

Pause.

ROBERT: You know. All of them. Bloody shits . . .

JOHN: What about them?

ROBERT: Why can they not leave us alone? *(Pause.)* Eh?

JOHN: Yes.

ROBERT: What? Eh?

JOHN: Yes.

ROBERT: You're damn right. *(Sotto voce)* Boring lunatics . . .

Scene 11

Onstage.

JOHN: Oh, the autumn.

Pause.

ROBERT: Yes.

JOHN: Autumn weather.

ROBERT: Yes.

JOHN: Oh, for the sun.

ROBERT: Will you pass me my robe, please?

JOHN: Your laprobe.

ROBERT: Yes. *(Business.)*

JOHN: Maman says just one more day, one more day, yet another week.

ROBERT: Mmm.

JOHN: One more week.

ROBERT: Would you please close the window?

JOHN: What? I'm sorry?

ROBERT: Do you feel a draft?

JOHN: A slight draft, yes. *(Pause.)* Shall I close the window?

ROBERT: Would you mind?

JOHN: No, not at all. (I love this window.) *(Pause.) (Closes the window.)*

ROBERT: Thank you.

JOHN: Mmm.

ROBERT: This room . . . this room.

JOHN: If we could leave this afternoon.

ROBERT: Mmm?

JOHN: If we could just call . . . bring the carriage round, just leave this afternoon . . .

ROBERT: It's much too cold . . .

JOHN: Just throw two shirts into a bag . . . a scarf . . .

ROBERT: (. . . the roads . . .)

JOHN: Just meet the train. *(Pause.)* Venice . . .

> *Pause.*

ROBERT: It's much too cold.

> *Pause.*

JOHN: Would you like a glass of tea?

ROBERT: What? Thank you, yes.

JOHN: I like this room.

ROBERT: Yes, so do I.

JOHN: I always have.

Pause.

ROBERT: So have I.

JOHN: I'll ring for tea.

Pause.

ROBERT: Thank you.

Scene 12

Backstage. ROBERT *and* JOHN *changing clothes.*

ROBERT: I wish they'd wash this stuff more often.

JOHN: Mmm.

ROBERT: Smells like a gym in here.

JOHN: The building's old.

ROBERT: Yes. Yes. *(Pause.)* Tired?

JOHN: No. A little.

ROBERT: Mmm.

Scene 13

JOHN *and* ROBERT *are sitting and reading a new script.*

ROBERT: Good. All right. Got a match?

JOHN *lights* ROBERT*'s cigarette.*

Mmm. Thank you.

JOHN: Mmm.

ROBERT: All right. Good. *(Starts reading)* "One day blends into the next" ... I'm not going to do the accent. Eh?

JOHN: Yes.

ROBERT: Good. One day blends into the next. Scorching sun ... shiv'ring moon. Salt ... saltwater....

JOHN: "It'll rain soon" ...　　ROBERT *(musing):* Salt ...
I'm sorry?　　　　　　　　　saltwater ...

ROBERT: Eh?

JOHN: I'm sorry. What?

56 •

ROBERT: No, I'm just thinking. Salt. Saltwater. Eh? The thought. He lets you see the thought there.

Pause.

JOHN: Mmm.

Pause.

ROBERT: Salt! Sweat. His life flows out. *(Pause.)* Then salt*water!* Eh?

JOHN: Yes.

ROBERT: To the *sea.*

JOHN: Yes.

ROBERT: All right. Good.

THEY *go back.*

"One day blends into the next. Salt. Saltwater."

JOHN: "It'll rain soon."

ROBERT: "Rain? What do *you* know about it?" *(Pause.)* "I've spent my whole life on the sea, and all that I know is the length of my ignorance. Which is *complete*, sonny." *(Pause.)* "My ignorance is complete."

JOHN: "It's gotta rain."

ROBERT: The motif, eh, the leitmotif. He takes the descant through the scene—"It's got to rain." You look at it, he does the same thing through the play.

Pause.

JOHN: Mmm.

ROBERT: Go on.

Pause.

JOHN: "It's gotta rain."

ROBERT: "Tell it to the marines."

JOHN: "It doesn't rain, I'm going off my nut."

ROBERT: You see: it *will* rain, it's *got* to rain, it *doesn't* rain. . . . all right, all right. "Just take it easy, kid . . . what you don't want to do now is sweat." *(Pause.)* "Believe me."

Pause.

JOHN: "We're never getting out of this alive." *(Pause.)* "Are we?"

ROBERT: "How do you want it?"

JOHN: "Give it to me straight."

Pause.

ROBERT: "Kid, we haven't got a chance in hell." *(Pause. Musing)* "We haven't got a chance in hell. We're never getting out of this alive." *(Pause.)* Eh? He sets it on the sea, we are marooned, he tells us that the sea is life, and then we're never getting out of it alive. *(Pause.)* Eh?

Pause.

JOHN: Yes.

ROBERT: The man could write.... All right. All right. *(Pause.)* Let's go back a bit.

Pause.

JOHN *(sighs):* "It'll rain soon. . ."

Scene 14

ROBERT *and* JOHN *are eating Chinese food at the makeup table between shows.*

ROBERT: You had an audition this afternoon, eh?

JOHN: Yes.

ROBERT: How did it go?

JOHN: Well, I thought.

ROBERT: Yes?

   Pause.

JOHN: They were receptive. I thought it went well.

ROBERT: How did you feel?

JOHN: I felt good; they liked it.

ROBERT: That's nice.

JOHN: I thought so.

ROBERT: That's very nice. *(Pause. Eating)* There are two classes of phenomena.

JOHN: There are.

Pause.

ROBERT: There are those things we *can* control and those things which we cannot.

JOHN: Mmm.

ROBERT: You can't control what someone thinks of you.

JOHN: No.

ROBERT: That is up to them. They may be glum, they may be out-of-sorts. Perhaps they are neurotic.

JOHN: How's your duck?

ROBERT: Fine. *(Pause.)* One *can* control, however, one's actions. One's intentions.

JOHN: Pass the bread, please.

ROBERT: That is all one can control.

JOHN: Please pass the bread.

ROBERT: You're eating bread?

JOHN: Yes.

ROBERT: Oh. *(Pause.)* Here it is.

JOHN: Thanks.

ROBERT: If they hadn't liked you, that would not have signified that you weren't a good actor.

JOHN: No. I think I know that.

ROBERT: Yes. I think perhaps you do. *(Pause.)* Yes. I'm glad they liked you, though.

JOHN: Thank you.

ROBERT: You think they're going to hire you?

JOHN: I don't know.

ROBERT: Well, I hope they do.

JOHN: I hope so, too.

ROBERT: That would be nice for you.

JOHN: Yes.

Pause.

ROBERT *(to self)*: Good things for good folk.

Scene 15

JOHN *and* ROBERT *are dressing backstage.*

ROBERT: We should do this whole frigging thing in rehearsal clothes, you know? Eh? Do it in blue jeans and T-shirts and give it some life, you know?

JOHN: Yes.

ROBERT: Eh? And give it some *guts. (Pause.)* Give *guts* to it. *(Pause.)* And to hell with experimentation. Artistic experimentation is shit. Huh?

JOHN: Right.

ROBERT: You're frigging well told. *(Pause.)* Two *actors,* some *lines* . . . and an audience. That's what I say. Fuck 'em all.

Scene 16

Onstage. The Barricades.

ROBERT: And the people cry for truth; the people cry for freedom from the vicious lies and slanders of the ages . . . the slanders of the body and the soul. The heart cries out: the memory says man has always lived in chains . . . has always lived in chains . . . *(Pause.)* Bread, bread, bread, the people scream . . . we drown their screaming with our heads in cups, in books . . . in newspapers . . . between the breasts of women . . . in our work . . . enough. A new day rises . . . those who must connect themselves to yesterday for succor will be left behind . . . their souls are in the histories, their heads on pikes around the buildings of our government. Now we must look ahead. . . . Our heads between the breasts of women, plight our troth to that security far greater than protection of mere rank or fortune. Now: we must dedicate ourselves to spirit: to the spirit of humanity; to life. *(Pause.)* To the barricades! *(Pause.)* Bread, bread, bread.

Scene 17

At the makeup table.

ROBERT: A makeup table. Artificial light. The scent of powder. Tools. Sticks. Brushes. Tissues. *(Pause.)* Cold *cream. (Pause.)* Greasepaint. *(Pause.)* Greasepaint! What is it? Some cream base, some coloring . . . texture, smell, color . . . analyze it and what have you? Meaningless component parts, though one could likely say the same for anything. . . . *But* mix and package it, affix a label, set it on a makeup table . . . a brush or two . . .

JOHN: Would you please shut up?

Pause.

ROBERT: Am I disturbing you?

JOHN: You are.

Pause.

ROBERT: Enough to justify this breach of etiquette?

JOHN: What breach? What etiquette?

ROBERT: John . . .

JOHN: Yes?

ROBERT: When one's been in the theatre as long as I . . .

JOHN: Can we do this later?

ROBERT: I feel that there is something here of worth to you.

JOHN: You do?

ROBERT: Yes.

JOHN *(sighs):* Let us hear it then.

ROBERT: All right. You know your attitude, John, is not of the best. It isn't. It just isn't.

JOHN *(Pause):* It isn't?

ROBERT: Forms. The Theatre's a closed society. Constantly abutting thoughts, the feelings, the emotions of our colleagues. Sensibilities *(pause)* bodies . . . *forms* evolve. An etiquette, eh? In our personal relations with each other. Eh, John? In our personal relationships.

Pause.

JOHN: Mmm.

ROBERT: One generation sows the seeds. It instructs the preceding . . . that is to say, the *following* generation . . . from the quality of its actions. Not from its discourse, John, no, but organically. *(Pause.)* You can learn a lot from keeping your mouth shut.

JOHN: You can.

ROBERT: Yes. And perhaps this is not the place to speak of attitudes.

JOHN: Before we go on.

ROBERT: Yes. But what is "life on stage" but attitudes?

JOHN *(Pause):* What?

ROBERT: Damn little.

Pause.

JOHN: May I use your brush?

ROBERT: Yes. *(Hands* JOHN *brush.)* One must speak of these things, John, or we will go the way of all society.

JOHN: Which is what?

ROBERT: Take too much for granted, fall away and die. *(Pause.)* On the boards, or in society at large. There must be law, there must be a reason, there must be tradition.

Pause.

JOHN: I'm sorry that I told you to shut up.

ROBERT: No, you can't buy me off that cheaply.

JOHN: No?

ROBERT: No.

Pause.

JOHN: Would you pass me the cream, please?

ROBERT: Certainly. *(Passes the cream.)* Here is the cream.

JOHN: Thank you.

Scene 18

Onstage. The famous lifeboat scene.

ROBERT: One day blends into the next. Scorching sun, shivering moon. Salt. Saltwater . . .

JOHN: It'll rain soon.

ROBERT: Rain. . . ? What do *you* know about it? *(Pause.)* I've spent my whole life on the sea, and all that I know is the length of my ignorance. Which is *complete*, sonny. *(Pause.)* My ignorance is complete.

JOHN: It's gotta rain.

ROBERT: Tell it to the marines.

JOHN: It doesn't rain, I'm going off my nut.

ROBERT: Just take it easy, kid. . . . What you don't wanna do now is sweat. *(Pause.)* Believe me.

Pause.

JOHN: We're never getting out of this alive. *(Pause.)* Are we?

ROBERT: How do you want it?

JOHN: Give it to me straight.

ROBERT: Kid, we haven't got a chance in hell. *(Pause.)* But you know what? *(Pause.)* You shouldn't let it get you down. And you know why? 'Cause that's the gamble. That's what life on the sea is about.

JOHN: Can I tell you something?

ROBERT: Shoot.

JOHN: You're full of it, I mean it. Don't you tell me about Men and the Sea, because that's been out of the picture for years. If it ever existed. No, it probably did. Back in the days when a man had a stake in what he went out after, when he had a stake in his ship . . . and a stake in himself. . . . But *now* . . . Now we're dyin' 'cause some black bastard shipowner in Newport decided that rather than make his ships safe for men, it was cheaper to overinsure them. *(Pause.)* THAT'S what we're dying for . . .

Pause. The KID *breaks down.*

ROBERT: Danny . . . Danny . . . A ship!!! *A SHIP!!!*

Scene 19

JOHN and ROBERT are standing in the wings. JOHN is about to go on.

ROBERT: Ephemeris, ephemeris, eh?

JOHN: What?

ROBERT: Ephemeris, ephemeris.

Pause.

JOHN: What are you saying?

ROBERT: Time passes.

Pause.

JOHN: What comes after: "The men got together, ma'am, and we kind of thought you'd like to have this"?

ROBERT: She says, "Thank you."

JOHN: I'm aware of that, I think. *After* that. What comes after that?

ROBERT: Your line?

JOHN: Yes.

ROBERT: Uh . . .

JOHN: Have you got a script?

ROBERT: What would I be doing with a script?

JOHN: I'm going to go get a script.

ROBERT: Wait. I know what the line is. . . .

JOHN: What?

ROBERT: Uh, after you give her the watch, right?

JOHN: Yes.

ROBERT: Right. You give her the *watch*. You give her the
watch . . .

JOHN: And?

ROBERT: Ah, Christ . . . you hand the cunt the watch:
"Ma'am, we kinda thought that maybe . . ."

JOHN: "The men all got together, ma'am . . ."

ROBERT: Yes. And . . . um . . . this is ridiculous . . . You
give her the *watch* . . . (What's *her* line?)

JOHN: "Thank you."

   Pause.

ROBERT: Ah, fuck. You'd better get a script. You want me
to?

JOHN: Sshhhhh!

   Pause.

ROBERT: What?

JOHN: Shut up. I'm trying to hear my cue.

Pause.

ROBERT: What's happening?

Pause.

JOHN: I think I missed my cue. *(Pause.)* I think I missed my *cue.*

Pause.

ROBERT: What's happening?

JOHN: Sshhhhhhh!

ROBERT: Can you see?

JOHN: I'm going on. *(Pause.)* I'm going to go on. *(Pause).* What do you think?

ROBERT *shrugs. Pause.*

Christ. I'm going out. . . .

ROBERT: You want me to get a script?

JOHN: I've missed my cue. . . . I've missed my cue. . . .

ROBERT: Well, go out there . . . go on.

Pause.

JOHN: Oh, God. I've missed my cue. . . .

ROBERT: Get *out* there. . . .

JOHN *(making his entrance):* "Missus Wilcox??? Missus Wilcox, ma'am? The men all got together. . . ."

Scene 20

Backstage. JOHN *is dressing.* ROBERT *enters, speaking slowly to himself.*

ROBERT: Oh God, oh God, oh God, oh God, oh God. *(He sees* JOHN. *Pause.)* New sweater?

JOHN: Yes.

ROBERT: Nice.

JOHN: Mmm.

ROBERT: What is it?

JOHN: What?

ROBERT: What is it? Cashmere?

JOHN: I don't know.

ROBERT: Looks good on you.

JOHN: Thanks.

ROBERT: Mmm.

Scene 21

Backstage. JOHN *is at the telephone, waiting.* ROBERT *enters.*

ROBERT: And everybody wants a piece. They all have got to get a piece.

JOHN (*into phone*): I'll wait.

ROBERT: We spend our adult lives bending over for incompetents. For ten-percenters, sweetheart unions, everybody in the same bed together. Agents. All the bloodsuckers. The robbers of the cenotaph. Who are we?

JOHN: Who? (*into phone*) Hello?

ROBERT: Who indeed?

JOHN: I'm holding for Miss Erenstein.

ROBERT: If we cannot speak to each other . . . what do we have but our fellow workers? If we do not have that, what do we have? Who can speak our language, eh?

JOHN (*to* ROBERT): And what of talent?

ROBERT: And what of it? *(Pause.)* What of humanity?

> *Pause.*

JOHN: What?

ROBERT: I don't know. *(Pause.)* Let's get a drink.

JOHN: I'm on the phone.

ROBERT: Hang it up.

JOHN *(into phone):* Hello, Bonnie? *John.* How *are* you . . . ?

ROBERT: We enslave ourselves.

JOHN *(into phone): No!*

ROBERT: (God.)

JOHN *(into phone):* Why, *thank* you. Thank you very much. *(Pause.)* On the *film* . . . ? Yes? Yes? I'll check my book.

ROBERT: One does not have to check one's "book" to get a *drink. (To himself)* A drink cannot buy *itself.*

JOHN *(covering phone):* Do you know who this *is?*

ROBERT: I am going to drink. For I must drink now. Do you know why?

JOHN: Why?

> *Pause.*

ROBERT: It is fitting. *(Exits.)*

JOHN *(into phone):* Yes. Eleven's *fine. (Pause.)* Wonderful.

Scene 22

Backstage. ROBERT *and* JOHN *are taking off their makeup.*

ROBERT: Fucking leeches.

JOHN: Mmm. Pass me the tissue, please?

ROBERT: They'll praise you for the things you never did and pan you for a split second of godliness. What do they know? They create nothing. They come in the front door. They don't even buy a ticket.

JOHN: No.

ROBERT: They've praised you too much. I do not mean to detract from your reviews—you deserve praise, John, much praise.

JOHN: Thank you.

ROBERT: Not, however, for those things which they have praised you for.

JOHN: In your opinion.

ROBERT: Yes, John, yes. From now on. *(Pause)*. You must be very careful who you listen to. From whom you take advice.

JOHN: Yes.

ROBERT: Never take *advice* . . .

JOHN: Yes . . .

ROBERT: . . . from *people* . . .

JOHN: May I have my comb, please?

ROBERT: . . . who do not have a vested interest, John, in your eventual success.

JOHN: I won't.

ROBERT: Or, barring that, in Beauty in the Theatre.

JOHN: I thought that they were rather to the point.

ROBERT: You did.

JOHN: Yes.

ROBERT: Your reviews.

JOHN: Yes.

ROBERT: All false modesty aside.

JOHN: Yes.

ROBERT: Oh, the Young, the Young, the Young, the Young.

JOHN: The Farmer in the Dell.

ROBERT: Oh, I see.

JOHN: Would you hand me my scarf, please?

Pause.

ROBERT: You fucking TWIT.

JOHN: I beg your pardon?

ROBERT: I think that you heard me. *(Takes towel from JOHN's area and begins to use it.)*

Pause.

JOHN: Robert.

ROBERT: What?

JOHN: Use your own towels from now on.

ROBERT: They're at the laundry.

JOHN: Get them back.

Scene 23

A dark stage, One worklight lit. JOHN *is rehearsing.*

JOHN: Now all the youth of England are on fire
And silken dalliance in the wardrobe lies.
Now thrive the Armourers and honor's thought
Reigns solely in the breast of every man.

ROBERT *(offstage):* Ah, sweet poison of the actor, rehearsing in an empty theatre upon an empty stage . . .

JOHN: Good evening.

ROBERT: . . . but full of life, full of action, full of resolve, full of youth. *(Pause.)* Please continue. *(Pause.)* Please, please continue. I'd like you to. . . . I'm sorry. Does this upset you? Does it upset you that someone is watching? I'm sorry, I can understand that. *(Pause.)* It's good. It's *quite* good. I was watching you for a while. I hope you don't mind. Do you mind?

JOHN: I've only been here a minute or so.

ROBERT: And I've watched you all that time. It seemed so long. It was so full. You're very good, John. Have I told you that lately? You are becoming a very fine actor. The flaws of youth are the perquisite of the young. It is the perquisite of the young to possess the flaws of youth.

JOHN: It's fitting, yes. . . .

ROBERT: Ah, don't mock me, John. You shouldn't mock me. It's too easy. It's not good for you, no. And that is a lesson which we have to learn. *(Pause.)* Which you have to learn.

JOHN: And what is that?

ROBERT: That it is a hurtful fault, John, to confuse sincerity with weakness. *(Pause.)* And I must tell you something.

JOHN: Yes.

ROBERT: About the Theatre—and this is a wondrous thing about the Theatre—and John, one of the ways in which it's most like life . . .

JOHN: And what is that?

Pause.

ROBERT: Simply this. That in the *Theatre* (as in life—and the Theatre is, of course, a *part* of life . . . No?) . . . Do you see what I'm saying? I'm saying, as in a grocery store, that you cannot separate the *time* one spends . . . that is, it's all part of one's *life. (Pause.)* In addition to the fact that what's happening on *stage* is life . . . of a sort . . . I mean, it's part of your *life. (Pause.)* Which is one reason I'm so *gratified* (if I may presume, and I recognize that it may be a presumption) to see you . . . to see the *young* of the Theatre . . . (And it's *not* unlike one's children) . . .

following in the footpaths of . . . following in the footsteps of . . . those who have gone before. *(Pause.)* Do you see what I am saying? I would like to think you *did*. Do you? John? *(Pause.)* Well . . . well. Goodnight, John.

Pause.

JOHN: Goodnight.

ROBERT: *Good*night. I'll see you.

HE *waves, starts to exit.*

JOHN: *Good* night. *(Long pause.)*

JOHN *examines the wings where* ROBERT *has exited.* JOHN *takes the stage.*

They sell the pasture now to buy the horse
Following the mirror of all Christian Kings
With the winged heels as English Mercuries.

Pause.

For now sits Expectation in the air

Pause.

And hides a sword.

Pause. HE *talks into the wings*

Are you back in there? Robert? Are you back in there? *(Pause.)* I *see* you in there. I see you there, Robert.

ROBERT *(offstage voice):* I'm just leaving.

JOHN: You were not just leaving, you were . . . *looking* at me.

ROBERT: On my way *out*, John. On my way *out*. Christ, but you make me feel small. You make me feel *small*, John. I don't feel good.

Pause.

JOHN: Are you crying? Are you crying, Robert, for chrissakes? *(Pause.) Christ.* Are you crying?

ROBERT: Yes.

Pause.

JOHN: Well, stop *crying*.

ROBERT: Yes. I will.

JOHN: No, stop it *now*. Stop it. Please.

Pause. ROBERT *stops crying.*

ROBERT: Better?

Pause.

JOHN: Yes. *(Pause).* Are you all right?

ROBERT: Oh, yes. I'm all right. I'm fine. Thank you, John. *(Pause.)* Well, I suppose I'll ... (You're going to work summore, eh?)

JOHN: Yes.

ROBERT: Then I suppose I'll.... (Well, I was leaving *anyway*.) *(Pause.)* Goodnight. Goodnight, John.

Pause.

JOHN: Are you all right now? *(raising his voice)* Robert! Are you all right now?

ROBERT *(far offstage):* Yes. Thank you. Yes. I'm all right now.

Pause.

JOHN *takes the stage again, is about to begin declaiming.*

ROBERT *(from far offstage):* You're not angry with me, are you?

JOHN: No.

ROBERT: You're sure?

JOHN: Yes.

Pause.

ROBERT: I'm glad, John. *(Pause.)* Thank you.

JOHN: Goodnight, Robert. *(Pause.)* Robert? *(Pause.)*

JOHN *takes the stage.*

Now all the Youth of England are on fire. . .

Pause.

Robert?

Pause.

ROBERT: Yes, John?

JOHN: Are you out there?

ROBERT: Yes, John.

JOHN *(sotto voce):* Shit.

Scene 24

Onstage. ROBERT *and* JOHN *are dressed in surgical smocks, and stand behind a form on an operating table.*

ROBERT: Give me some suction there, doctor, will you . . . that's good.

JOHN: Christ, what I wouldn't give for a cigarette.

ROBERT: Waaal, just a few more minutes and I think I'll join you in one. *(Pause.)* Nervous, Jimmy?

JOHN: No. Yes.

ROBERT: No need to be. A few years, you'll be doing these in your sleep. Suction. Retractor. *(Business.)* No, the *large* retractor.

JOHN: Sorry.

ROBERT: It's all right. Give me another one, will you?

(Business)

JOHN *(pointing)*: What's that?

Pause. ROBERT *shakes his head minutely.* JOHN *nods his head.*

What's that?

ROBERT *minutely but emphatically shakes his head.*

Pause.

JOHN *mumbles something to* ROBERT. ROBERT *mumbles something to* JOHN.

Pause.

ROBERT: Would you, uh, can you give me some sort of reading on the, uh, electro ... um ... on the .... Would you get me one, please? *(motioning* JOHN *offstage)* No ... on the, uh ... would you get me a reading on this man?

JOHN *(pointing):* What's *that!!!?*

ROBERT: What is what? Eh?

JOHN: What's that near his spleen? *(Pause.)* A curious growth near his spleen?

ROBERT: What?

JOHN: A Curious Growth Near His Spleen? *(Pause.)* Is that one, there?

ROBERT: No, I think not. I think you cannot see a growth near his spleen for some *time* yet. So would you (as this man's in shock) ... would you get me, please, give me a reading on his vital statements. Uh, *Functions. . . ?* Would you do that one thing for me, please?

JOHN *(sotto voce):* We've done that one, Robert.

ROBERT: I fear I must disagree with you, Doctor. Would you give me a reading on his vital *things*, if you please? Would you? *(Pause.)* For the love of God?

JOHN *(sotto voce):* That's in the other part.

ROBERT: No, it is *not*. He's in shock. He's in shock, and I'm becoming miffed with you. Now: if you desire to work in this business again, will you give me a reading? If you wish to continue here inside the hospital? *(Pause.)* Must I call a *policeman!!*? *(Pause.)* Have you no feeling? This man's in deepest shock!!!

Pause. JOHN *takes off his mask and walks away.*

And now where are you going? *(Pause.)* You *quitter!!*

(Another pause.) (To audience)

Ladies and gentlemen. What we have seen here today is—I won't say a *"perfect"*—but a very good example of successful surgical technique, performed under modern optimum conditions, uh . . . and with a minimum of *fuss* . . . a minimum of *mess* and *bother* . . . and I hope that you have . . . *(The curtain is being rung down on him)* . . . that you have found it every bit. . . .

Curtain is down. Hold.

ROBERT *(generally):* Does anybody have a script?

Scene 25

Backstage. ROBERT *appears, holding his left wrist with his right hand.*

ROBERT: Oh God, oh God, I've cut myself.

JOHN *(entering):* What have you done?

ROBERT: I'm bleeding. Oh, my God . . .

JOHN: Christ.

ROBERT: What a silly accident. Can you believe this?

JOHN: Come on.

ROBERT: Where?

JOHN: We're going to the hospital.

ROBERT: Oh, no. Oh no. I'm all right, really.

JOHN: Come on.

ROBERT: No. What would they say? Kidding aside. *(Pause.)* No. I'm quite all right. My razor slipped and now I'm fine. I had a moment, though. I did. *(Pause.)* John . . . *(Pause.)* John . . .

JOHN: Yes?

ROBERT: Did you know in olden times they used to say "clean-shaven like an actor"? *(Pause.)* Did you know that?

JOHN: Are you all right?

ROBERT: Oh, yes. I'm fine. I've lost a little blood is all. It's nothing, really. *(Pause.)* A mishap. *(Pause.)* Clean-shaven . . .

JOHN: God, what's wrong with you?

ROBERT: There's nothing wrong with me. My hand slipped. *(Pause.)* I'm tired. That's all. I'm tired. *(Pause.)* I need to rest. We all need rest. We all need rest. It's much too much. It's just too much. I'm tired. *(Pause.)* You understand? I'm *tired.*

JOHN: Well, I'm calling you a doctor.

ROBERT: No. You're not. No. Please. I'm only tired. I'm going to go home. I'm only tired. We think we see things clearly when we haven't enough sleep. But we do not. I've cut myself. I've dirtied up the basin. *(Pause.)* I'm going to go home now.

JOHN: I'll come home with you.

ROBERT: No. Thank you. I'll get home alone. I only have to rest now. Thank you. *(Pause.)* But thank you all the same.

JOHN: I'll take you home.

ROBERT: What? No. I think I'm only going to sit here for

a moment. *(Pause.)* I'll be all right. I'll be all right tomorrow. I'll be my old self. I'm all right *now.* *(Smiles.)* *(Pause.)* I'm only going to rest a moment . . . and then I'll go home.

JOHN *looks to* ROBERT *for a moment, then exits.* ROBERT *remains onstage alone for a moment, then slowly exits.*

Scene 26

Backstage, after a show.

ROBERT: I loved the staircase scene tonight.

JOHN: You did?

ROBERT: Just like a poem.

Pause.

JOHN: I thought the execution scene worked beautifully.

ROBERT: No. You *didn't.*

JOHN: Yes. I did.

Pause.

ROBERT: *Thank* you. Getting cold, eh?

JOHN: Yes.

ROBERT *(to himself):* It's getting cold. *(Aloud)* You know, my father always wanted me to be an actor.

JOHN: Yes?

ROBERT: Always wanted me to be . . .

Pause.

JOHN: Well! (*Crosses and picks up umbrella.*)

ROBERT: It's raining?

JOHN: I think it will. You got a fag?

ROBERT: Yes. Always wanted me to be.

ROBERT *hands* JOHN *a cigarette.*

JOHN: Thank you.

ROBERT: Mmm.

JOHN: Got a match?

ROBERT: You going out?

JOHN: Yes.

ROBERT: Where? A party?

JOHN: No. I'm going with some people.

ROBERT: Ah.

JOHN: You have a match?

ROBERT: No.

JOHN *hunts for a match on the makeup table.*

JOHN: Are you going out tonight?

ROBERT: I don't know; I suppose so.

JOHN: Mmm.

ROBERT: I'm not eating too well these days.

JOHN: No, eh?

ROBERT: No.

JOHN: Why?

ROBERT: Not hungry.

> JOHN *picks up matchbook, struggles to light match.*

> I'll get it.

JOHN: Do you mind?

ROBERT: No.

> ROBERT *takes matchbook and lights* JOHN's *cigarette.*

JOHN: Thank you.

> *Pause.*

ROBERT: A life spent in the theatre.

JOHN: Mmm.

ROBERT: Backstage.

JOHN: Yes.

ROBERT: The bars, the house, the drafty halls. The penciled scripts . . .

JOHN: Yes.

ROBERT: Stories. Ah, the stories that you hear.

JOHN: I know.

ROBERT: It all goes so fast. It goes so quickly.

> *Long pause.*

JOHN: You think that I might borrow twenty 'til tomorrow?

ROBERT: What, you're short on cash?

JOHN: Yes.

ROBERT: Oh. Oh. *(Pause.)* Of course. *(He digs in his pocket. Finds money and hands it to* JOHN.*)*

JOHN: You're sure you won't need it?

ROBERT: No. No, not at all. No. If I don't know how it is, who does?

Pause.

JOHN: Thank you.

ROBERT: Mmm. Goodnight.

JOHN: Goodnight.

ROBERT: You have a nice night.

JOHN: I will.

ROBERT: Goodnight.

> JOHN *exits. Pause.*
>
> Ephemeris, ephemeris. *(Pause.)* "An actor's life for me."
>
> ROBERT *composes himself and addresses the empty house.* HE *raises his hand to stop imaginary applause.*
>
> You've been so kind . . . Thank you, you've really been so kind. You know, and I speak, I am sure, not for myself alone, but on behalf of all of us . . . *(composes himself)* . . . All of us here, when I say that

these . . . *these* moments make it all . . . they make it all worthwhile.

Pause. JOHN *quietly reappears.*

You know . . .

ROBERT *sees* JOHN.

JOHN: They're locking up. They'd like us all to leave.

ROBERT: I was just leaving.

JOHN: Yes, I know, *(Pause.)* I'll tell them.

ROBERT: Would you?

JOHN: Yes.

Pause.

ROBERT: Thank you.

JOHN: Goodnight.

ROBERT: Goodnight.

Pause.

JOHN *exits.*

ROBERT *(to himself):* The lights dim. Each to his own home. Goodnight. Goodnight. Goodnight.

OTHER GROVE PRESS DRAMA AND THEATER PAPERBACKS

17016-X ARDEN, JOHN / Plays: One (Serjeant Musgave's Dance, The Workhouse Donkey, Armstrong's Last Goodnight) / $4.95
17208-6 BECKETT, SAMUEL / Endgame / $2.95
17233-7 BECKETT, SAMUEL / Happy Days / $2.95
17204-3 BECKETT, SAMUEL / Waiting for Godot / $3.50
17112-8 BRECHT, BERTOLT / Galileo / $2.95
17472-0 BRECHT, BERTOLT / The Threepenny Opera / $2.45
17226-4 IONESCO, EUGENE / Rhinoceros and Other Plays (The Leader, The Future Is in Eggs, or It Takes All Sorts to Make a World) / $4.95
17016-4 MAMET, DAVID / American Buffalo / $4.95
17040-7 MAMET, DAVID / A Life in the Theatre / $6.95
17043-1 MAMET, DAVID / Sexual Perversity in Chicago and The Duck Variations / $5.95
17092-X ODETS, CLIFFORD / Six Plays (Waiting for Lefty; Awake and Sing; Golden Boy; Rocket to the Moon; Till the Day I Die; Paradise Lost) / $7.95
17001-6 ORTON, JOE / The Complete Plays (The Ruffian on the Stair, The Good and Faithful Servant, The Erpingham Camp, Funeral Games, Loot, What the Butler Saw, Entertaining Mr. Sloane) / $6.95
17251-5 PINTER, HAROLD / The Homecoming / $4.95
17885-8 PINTER, HAROLD / No Man's Land / $3.95
17539-5 POMERANCE, BERNARD / The Elephant Man / $4.25
17743-6 RATTIGAN, TERENCE / Plays: One / $5.95
17884-X STOPPARD, TOM / Travesties / $3.95
17260-4 STOPPARD, TOM / Rosencrantz and Guildenstern Are Dead / $3.95
17206-X WALEY, ARTHUR, tr. and ed. / The No Plays of Japan / $7.95

GROVE PRESS, INC., 196 West Houston St., New York, N.Y. 10014